ON FOOT (

NEW YORI

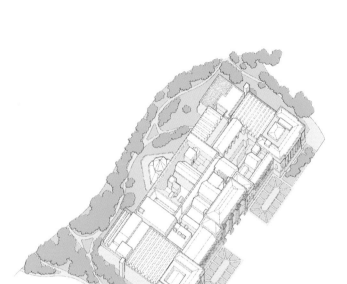

ON FOOT GUIDES

NEW YORK
WALKS

Jane Egginton

DUNCAN PETERSEN

Conceived, designed and produced by
Duncan Petersen Publishing Ltd

Editorial Director Andrew Duncan
Editors Fiona Duncan and Leonie Glass
Production Editor Nicola Davies
Art Director Mel Petersen
Designers Christopher Foley and Beverley Stewart

Maps Julian Baker
Photographs Helanna Bratman
Additional Photographs Jane Egginton

This edition published 2001 by
Duncan Petersen Publishing Ltd,
31 Ceylon Road, London W14 OPY

Sales representation and distribution in the U.K. and Ireland by Portfolio Books Limited
Unit 5, Perivale Industrial Park, Horsenden Lane South, Greenford
Mddx UB6 7RL
Tel: 020 8997 9000

ISBN 1-903301-16-5

A CIP catalogue record for this book is available from the British Library

Printed by Delo – Tiskarna, Slovenia
Origination by Mick Hodson and Associates

Thanks to Angela, Don, Heather and Helen

CONTENTS

Exploring New York on foot   6
  Location map   7
  How to use this book   7
  When to use this book   8-9
  Getting around   10-11
  Tourist information   11-15

THE WALKS:

Museum Mile: Upper East Side   16-23

A Landscaped Ramble: Central Park   24-31

Art and the Park: From Fifth Avenue to Central Park   32-39

A Shopping Spree: Madison and Fifth Avenues   40-47

West Side Story: From the Lincoln Center to Carnegie Hall   48-55

Bright Lights: Around Broadway   56-63

New York Giants: Around the Empire State Building   64-71

Leafy Bohemia: Greenwich Village   72-79

An East Village Evening: Around Second Avenue   80-87

Global Village: Around East Village   88-95

High Life: SoHo   96-103

A Gourmet Trail: Little Italy and Chinatown   104-111

On the Waterfront: To South Street Seaport   112-119

World Traders: Twin Towers to Battery Park   120-127

Exploring New York on foot

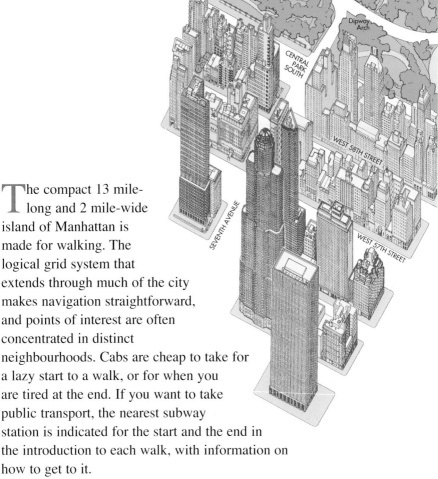

The compact 13 mile-long and 2 mile-wide island of Manhattan is made for walking. The logical grid system that extends through much of the city makes navigation straightforward, and points of interest are often concentrated in distinct neighbourhoods. Cabs are cheap to take for a lazy start to a walk, or for when you are tired at the end. If you want to take public transport, the nearest subway station is indicated for the start and the end in the introduction to each walk, with information on how to get to it.

The ariel-view (isometric) mapping used to illustrate all the walks make following the route interesting and easy. There is no need for complicated directions and sights and streets are brought to 3D life on the page. Points of interest to look out for are clearly marked on the map and on the page.

This guide takes in all the major sights of Manhattan and all the key areas. Even if you do not have time to do all the walks, reading them will give you an in-depth insight into the city. As well as giving you a commentary on the obvious tourist attractions, they will guide you to hidden places.

HOW TO USE THIS BOOK

The area covered by the walks stretches from Central Park in the
north to the southern tip of Manhattan, and the two 'villages'
of Greenwich and the East Village west to east.

Using the maps

The route taken by each walk is clearly marked on the
map with the occasional arrow to ensure you are
heading in the right direction. Boxes tell you where
the walk starts and finishes and the nearest subway
station, which is generally never more than a few
minutes' walk away.

Numerals on the maps match the numerals in
the text, highlighting places of interest and
importance. Where this is a specific building,
the numeral will appear on the building, but
where there are several places of interest in the
same street, the numeral will normally be placed
on the street.

From the
Lincoln Center to
Carnegie Hall
48-55

Central Park 24-31

Upper East Side
16-23

From Fifth
Avenue to
Central Park
32-39

Around
Broadway
56-63

Madison and
Fifth Avenues
40-47

Around the
Empire State
Building
64-71

Greenwich
Village
72-79

Around Second
Avenue 80-87

SoHo
96-103

Around East
Village
88-95

Little Italy and
Chinatown
104-111

Twin Towers
to Battery Park
120-127

To South
Street
Seaport
112-119

The place of interest appears in bold print in the text, which is also used to highlight other
significant places nearby, such as buildings, museums, galleries, statues, sculptures,
restaurants, cafés or shops. Opening times are given for sights, where relevant, so you can
organize and time your walk around a visit to one or several of these (for more information
on admissions to sights, see page 14).

LINKING THE WALKS

Many of the walks can be done in a few hours, depending on how much time you spend
looking at the points of interest along the way. Some of the routes have been designed to
link up with each other, so you can create your own longer version.

The end of **On the Waterfront** connects with **World Traders** if you follow St John
Street from the piers and turn right on to Broadway for St Paul's Chapel.

If you finish the short walk through SoHo, **High Life,** and fancy some food you are in
the right place to start **A Gourmet Trail** through Little Italy and Chinatown. Just walk
along Prince Street, turning down Lafayette Street for one block.

To combine the two 'village' walks, simply walk east along Washington Mews at the
finish of **Leafy Bohemia,** which explores Greenwich Village, to Astor Place and the start
of the East Village walk, **Global Village.** If you feel like an **East Village Evening**
cruising the bars and restaurants in this lively part of town, after either of these walks, it's
a short way down Fourth Avenue and left along East Fourth Street for one block for the
start of this after-dark tour.

Walk along 42nd Street from the Chrysler Building, the last point of interest on the
New York Giants route to Times Square if you want to begin the **Bright Lights** tour
around the theatre district to the Rockefeller Center.

A Shopping Spree ends where **Art and the Park** begins, allowing them to be easily
combined. The latter can be extended to include the galleries of **Museum Mile** with a
short and pleasant walk up East Drive through Central Park to the Frick Museum.

WHEN TO USE THIS BOOK

Most of the walks can be enjoyed at any time of the year, although the routes taking in Central Park and those areas where there is a vibrant street life are obviously much more enjoyable to do when the weather is fine. All the walks include a variety of points of interest such as museums, shops and other indoor attractions where you can take refuge from the weather if necessary.

SUMMER WALKS

A Landscaped Ramble: this walk through Central Park is ideal to do on a summer's day, stopping for ice cream at the Loeb Boathouse where you can hire a rowing boat.

On the Waterfront: exploring the exposed Brooklyn bridge and waterside area, with its outdoor museum, and a recommended boat trip are part of this walk, so it is best done in good weather.

Art and the Park: the second, Central Park, section around the zoo and the park's other features is much more enjoyable on a fine day.

New York Giants: although much of this walk looks at building interiors, the views

THE WEATHER

New York weather is prone to extremes and because of its island position can change very quickly. The city can be blisteringly hot in summer, and freezing with snow during the winter. The sunniest month is July, with an average top temperature of 84 degrees. Even during the winter the days are often bright. March and August have the most rain.

from the Empire State can be severely restricted on a foggy or cloudy day.

Leafy Bohemia: ideally a walk for a bright day, in order to enjoy a neighbourhood atmosphere where cafés spill on to the street.

WINTER WALKS

Museum Mile: numerous museums en route provide plenty of opportunity to take refuge from the elements if necessary.

A Shopping Spree: with the shops only a short hop away from each other, and many of them sprawling department stores, it is easy to take cover on this walk.

A Landscaped Ramble: Central Park in snow or frost is a magical experience. You can have a hot chocolate next to the frozen lake or take shelter in the mammoth American Museum of Natural History and the New Rose Center for Earth and Space at the end of the route.

West Side Story: the many buildings that make up the Lincoln Center provide indoor entertainment if the weather turns bad. The Russian Tea Room is a cosy place for tea at the walk's end.

HOW THE MAPPING WAS MADE

The mapping used in this book was originally created from specially commissioned photographs taken from a helicopter that flew at about 1,500 feet with the camera angled at 45 degrees. Weather conditions had to be slightly overcast in order to achieve maximum details on the buildings.

Scores of enlargements were made from negatives, which a group of technical illustrators then used to create the maps, working in pen and ink. For this book, the mapping has been developed further: extracted areas have been digitally redrawn and coloured.

WEEKEND WALKS

On the Waterfront: this is a lively place to be on weekends, when locals jog over the Brooklyn Bridge and wander around Pier 17 and its surrounding 'outdoor museum'.

WEEKDAY WALKS

World Traders: to see the World Trade Center and Wall Street at its active best go during the week when office workers and traders are part of the scene. The New York Stock Exchange is not open on weekends.

The High Life: SoHo is packed with locals during the weekend, making weekdays a more relaxed time to visit.

A Shopping Spree: New Yorkers love to shop, so avoid the times when they are out in force, such as weekends and lunchtimes.

Museum Mile: this stretch of museums is always popular, but visiting on weekdays (not Mondays when many are closed) allows you to avoid the weekend crowds.

WALKS FOR CHILDREN

The American Museum of Natural History and the New Rose Center for Earth and Space on **A Landscaped Ramble** are always popular with kids. This walk also features a castle discovery centre for children and boat rides on a lake. A zoo designed specifically for children is featured on the **Art and the Park** walk and **A Shopping Spree** includes three giant toy shops. **On the Waterfront**, with its boats and bridge crossing, will appeal to most youngsters.

9

GETTING AROUND

THE SUBWAY

All the walks have been devised with a convenient subway station in mind. Each one includes details of the nearest subway station and how to get to it.

Using the subway

Subway connections are not as convenient as they might be, so you might find yourself having to change lines one or more times. Although some visitors are nervous about using subway trains, they have a good record of safety and are generally efficient. It is the fastest and cheapest way of getting around during the day, although many people choose not to travel at night. After 10pm there are fewer trains and people, so you may prefer to take a taxi.

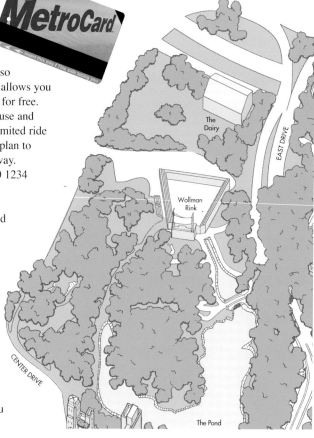

Subway fares

Buy a MetroCard or token for your journey from the booth at the subway entrance which are also valid for buses. A MetroCard allows you to change subways and buses for free. There are two kinds: pay per use and unlimited ride cards. The unlimited ride card is excellent value if you plan to travel extensively on the subway. (Contact the MTA on 718 330 1234 for more information.)

Each train has a letter or number, with the line indicated by colour coding. Green globes mark subway entrances and red globes indicate an entrance that is not always open. Check before paying whether you need the uptown or downtown platform. Check also whether the train is 'local' which will be slower or 'express' which may not stop at the station you require.

Many employees in America rely on tips to make up their very low wages. A 15 per cent tip is usually expected for taxi drivers and waiting staff. An easy way to work out the amount is to double the sales tax that appears on your bill. Bar staff, porters, hairdressers and maids should all be given a dollar or two.

BUSES

The advantage of travelling by bus is that you can continue sightseeing on your journey, although it will probably take longer than other methods of transport. Each blue and white vehicle displays the route number and destination digitally on the front. Buses stop every two blocks or so north and south, and each block east and west. Tourist information centres and subway stations supply bus maps.

CABS

The famous New York yellow taxis are cheap and normally easy to hail. You may have difficulty finding one late at night or in the rain – when traffic always seems to be twice as slow. Only cabs with their overhead light on are for hire, and will stop if you hold out an arm. Get in the car and then give directions, giving details of cross streets, rather than street numbers. The driving skills and route knowledge of New York cabbies are erratic and sometimes appalling. A tip of around 15 per cent is the norm unless you are unhappy with the service. If you do have any complaints the Taxi and Limousine Commission (tel. 212 302 8294) is the place to call, quoting the cab's licence plate number and the number displayed inside.

TOURIST INFORMATION

Most big hotels and major attractions have tourist information leaflets and maps. There are also visitor centres throughout the city. The New York Convention and Visitors Bureau at 810 Seventh Avenue at 53rd Street (tel. 800 692 8474) has extensive information and a telephone help line. The Times Square Visitors Information Bureau has a 24-hour phone service (tel. 800 692 8474).

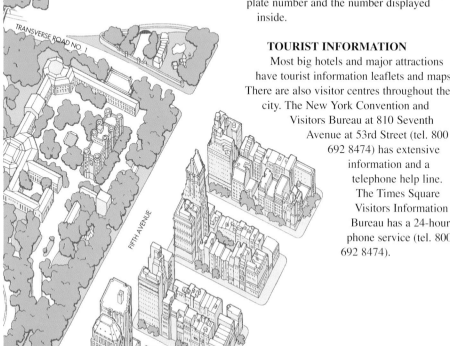

USEFUL TELEPHONE NUMBERS
Children
The Events for Children leaflet is worth getting hold of from local libraries, toy shops and other child-centred places. The Babysitters' Guild (tel. 212 682 0227) has a register of potential babysitters who speak 16 languages between them.

Disabled visitors
The Society for the Advancement of Travel for the Handicapped is a worldwide non-profit organization with its headquarters in New York. For information about membership call 212 447 7284. Many buses and hotels have wheelchair ramps and some of the museums have special tours for those who are deaf, blind or disabled. The Junior League of the City of New York has a directory of buildings that are accessible to the disabled (tel. 212 288 6220).

Sightseeing tours

Romantic horse-drawn carriages offer rides around Central Park from the Plaza Hotel at 59th Street and Fifth Avenue. For a bird's eye view of the city, try Liberty Helicopter Tours at West 30th Street and 12th Avenue (tel. 212 967 6464). The Circle Line offers popular boat tours. Take a three-hour trip around Manhattan from Pier 83 (tel. 212 563 3200) or a boat to the Statue of Liberty from Battery Park (tel. 212 269 5755).

Theatre tickets

For information about current shows on and Off-Broadway, pick up a copy of *Time Out* New York, the listings magazine, or the free *Village Voice*. NYC/On Stage (tel. 212 768 1818) is a phone line service with details of all theatre shows, as well as music and opera events.

You can buy most tickets easily over the phone with a credit card. Most shows throughout the city are represented by 24-hour ticket agencies, which provide the best way to buy tickets, as theatres generally don't take phone bookings. Ticketmaster (tel. 212 307 4100) and Telecharge (tel. 212 239 6200) are the two major companies. You will be charged a fee on top of the price of your tickets for this service.

TKTS is the major outlet for discounted tickets which sometimes has outstanding deals. There is a booth at the World Trade Center. Also for cheap tickets ask the theatre about standing room, or for standby tickets just before the show is due to start. Some theatres offer reductions for group bookings or two for the price of one deals.

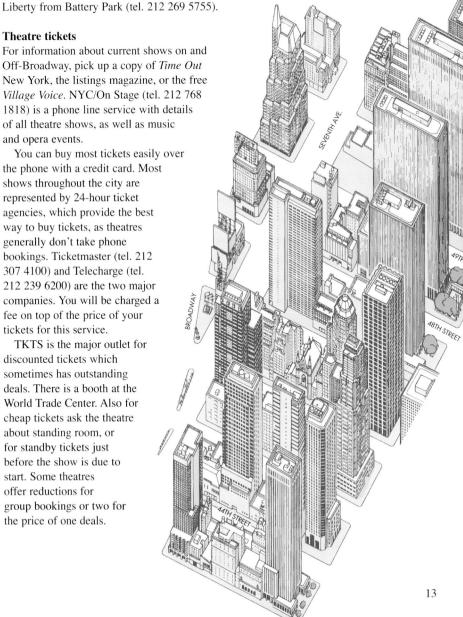

EMERGENCY INFORMATION

Dial 911 for the ambulance, fire or police service.

Emergency treatment
Call your insurance company first before seeking treatment to see which hospitals accept your kind of insurance. The following hospitals have emergency rooms:

Roosevelt Hospital
428 West 59th Street at Ninth Avenue (tel. 212 523 4000)

St Luke's Hosptial
1111 Amsterdam Avenue at 113th Street (tel. 212 604 7998)

You can also dial 411 and ask the operator for the number of the hospital most convenient for you.

Walk-in clinic
If you have a medical problem which is not serious, **DOCS** at 55 East 34th Street (tel. 212 252 6000) offers a walk-in service. It is open every day with extended hours. You will normally have to pay immediately.

Pharmacies

Duane Reade, 224 57th Street at Broadway (tel. 212 541 9708). This chain has branches throughout the city, some of which are open 24 hours.

Kaufman's at 557 Lexington Avenue at 50th Street is open until midnight (tel. 212 755 2266).

USEFUL WEBSITES

For up to date, easy to access information take a look at the following websites. All are searchable, and most have links to other related sites. Many hotels and even some shops have Internet access. There are Internet cafés throughout the city and the New York Public Library has reasonably priced Internet services (tel. 212 930 0747).

www.echonyc.com – for arts reviews and information about what to do in New York.

www.clubnyc.com – an online review of the city's club and nightlife scene.

www.nycvisit.com – this site for the New York Visitors Convention and Visitors Bureau has a variety of tourist information.

www.timeoutny.com – for listings and up-to-the-minute information about the city's events.

www.villagevoice.com – contains listings and other features from the free paper

www.whitehouse.gov – the official US government site.

Admissions and opening times
Business hours are normally between 9am and 5pm, although some banks close at 3pm. An entrance charge or required donation is normally charged by museums, although some do have free admission. Most close on Mondays and bank holidays, with late opening on one weekday.

Left luggage and lost property
If you lose something in the street call the police. The airports all have their own lost property offices. For buses and subways call the New York City Transit Authority (tel. 718 625 6200) and for items left in a taxi, call 212 221 8294.

SHOPPING AND BANKING HOURS

Shops downtown usually open later and close later than those in midtown. Late night shopping is on Thursday, when many outlets stay open until 7pm or even later. Banks are usually open between 9am and 3pm during the week. Bureaux de change stay open until around 7pm but charge commission and offer less favourable rates. Some hotels have 24-hour money exchange services, but again do not offer a good deal.

PUBLIC HOLIDAYS

Many attractions, public services, restaurants and even some shops do not shut down for public holidays, even Christmas Day.

However, banks and public offices and some places of interest close on the following public holidays: New Year's Day (1Jan), Martin Luther King Jr Day (third Mon in Jan), Presidents' Day (third Mon in Feb), Memorial Day (last Mon in May), Independence Day (4 July), Labour Day (first Mon in Sept), Columbus Day (second Mon in Oct), Election Day (first Tues after first Mon in Nov), Veterans' Day (11 Nov), Thanksgiving (fourth Thurs in Nov), Christmas Day (25 Dec).

WALKING SAFELY

Follow the 'walk'/'don't walk' indicators at pedestrian crossings. New York traffic waits for no one and jaywalking is illegal. At night avoid Central Park and any other park areas and always stick to well-lit streets. Don't forget that vehicles drive on the right. There are many one-way streets in the city so make a point of looking both ways before crossing.

16

Museum Mile: Upper East Side

This route takes in a unique concentration of museums on the Upper East Side, including the intimate Frick, the immense Metropolitan, and the often outrageously contemporary Whitney and Guggenheim Museums. Weave in and out of Central Park and up the most moneyed section of Fifth Avenue, taking a turn down ultra-rich Madison Avenue with its chic boutiques. Many of the museums have taken over the mansions of the turn-of-the-century millionaires who used to live here, and their architecture is often as distinctive as their art. Most have free audio and guided tours, are closed on Mondays and Sunday mornings, and open late on Tuesdays.

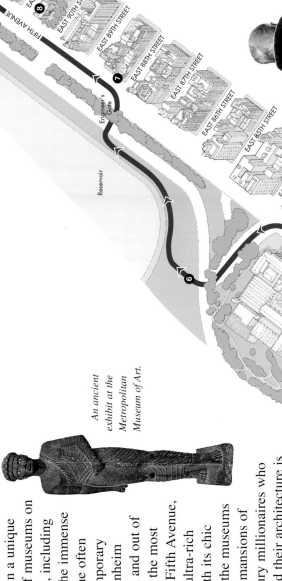

An ancient exhibit at the Metropolitan Museum of Art.

The Mad Hatter chuckles at the Alice in Wonderland sculpture.

ENDS

FIFTH AVENUE

EAST 92ND ST

EAST 91ST STREET

EAST 90TH STREET

EAST 89TH STREET

EAST 88TH STREET

EAST 87TH STREET

EAST 86TH STREET

EAST 85TH STREET

EAST 84TH STREET

EAST 83RD STREET

EAST 82ND STREET

Engineer's Gate

Reservoir

Metropolitan Museum of Art

▲ STARTS

Fifth Avenue and East 70th Street. Nearest subway 68th Street Hunter College at Lexington Avenue. Walk along East 68th Street for three blocks west and turn right on to Fifth Avenue. Walk two blocks to 70th St.

■ ENDS

Fifth Avenue and East 92nd Street. Nearest subway: 86th Street. Walk back down Fifth Avenue. Turn left on to 86th Street and follow it for three blocks; a 20-minute walk.

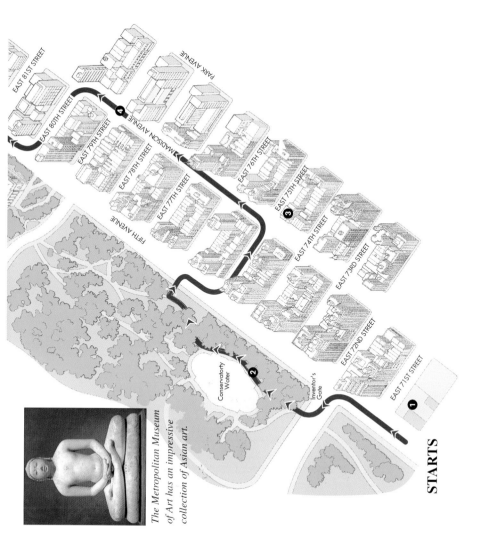

The Metropolitan Museum of Art has an impressive collection of Asian art.

STARTS

❶ Industrialist Henry Clay Frick was so fond of Renaissance art he filled his 1914 mansion with it, and left it for the world to enjoy when he died. The world-class art at the **Frick Collection** (1 East 70th Street), is arranged in different rooms of the house, with changing exhibitions. The mansion's interior with its French furniture and porcelains is sometimes as much on display as the art, creating a unique atmosphere, which can be intimate or stuffy depending on your point of view. The Dining Room and Library are devoted to English works like Thomas Gainsborough's *Mall in St James's Park* (1783). Rembrandt's *Portrait of a Young Artist* (1658) can be seen in the skylit West Gallery, with significant works by Van Dyck, Velázquez and Vermeer. No children under ten are admitted into the museum. (Closed Mon.)

The Model Boat Pond's glassy waters.

❷ Walk up Fifth Avenue to the statue of Samuel Morse, the New Yorker who sent the first telegraph message in 1837, standing at **Inventor's Gate**. At this entrance to Central Park, join the giant cherry trees overlooked by the suddenly distant grand apartments on Fifth Avenue. The lake-like **Conservatory Water**, more commonly known as the Model Boat Pond, is where hundreds of model boats take part in weekend races during the summer. Follow the path to the **Alice in Wonderland** sculpture in a magical woodland setting, which seems to invite enchanted children to clamber over it. Erected in memory of a wife who loved children, it features everyone from the Mad Hatter to the Cheshire Cat and is circled by quotes from Lewis Carroll's ever-popular book.

Samuel Morse statue.

Children love clambering over the Alice in Wonderland sculpture.

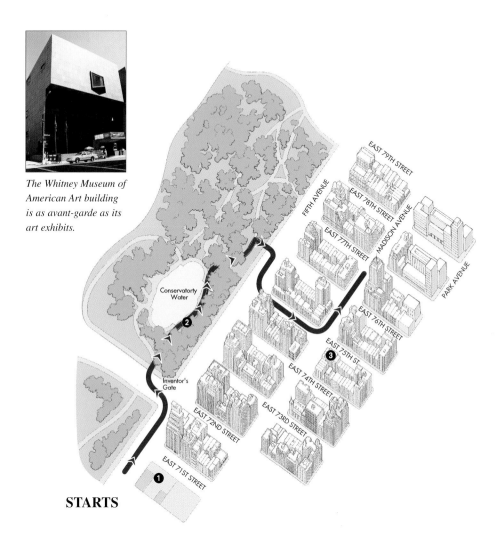

The Whitney Museum of American Art building is as avant-garde as its art exhibits.

STARTS

❸ Exit the park and walk down East 75th Street to the inverted granite pyramid of the **Whitney Museum of American Art** (closed Thurs am) which leans over the pavement at 945 Madison Avenue. Sculptor Gertrude Vanderbilt Whitney set up the museum in 1930 after the Metropolitan Museum of Art refused her collection, and dedicated it to living American artists. It now has 13,000 works, including some of Georgia O'Keeffe's best work and Edward Hopper's entire estate. Justly declaring itself the Advocate for 20thC American Art, the Whitney is perhaps best known for its controversial Biennial Exhibition every odd numbered year. Even the audio tours are radical, which may use a conversation with the artist and music instead of a formal commentary. Sarabeth's (tel. 212 570 3670) is popular for lunch.

MUSEUM MILE: UPPER EAST SIDE

❹ Stroll past **Madison Avenue's** jewellery shops, galleries and designer boutiques catering for the conservative tastes of their ridiculously rich clients. Look out for local celebrity residents like Joan Rivers, as well as dogwalkers circled with leashed apartment pets, and real estate brokers that look like palaces. This was an area once crowded with German and Irish immigrants, and the vibrant Latin American community of Spanish Harlem still thrives as close by as 96th Street.

❺ Dive back into Fifth Avenue at East 80th Street. The **Metropolitan Museum of Art** (open daily) has an overwhelming range of exhibits. Set up to rival national art institutions in Europe, its collections from all periods and all continents mean you have to be selective. Visit the second floor European painting and sculpture, thought by some to be at its heart, The Egyptian Collection, or the 20thC art. Alternatively, join one of the guided tours of the museum's highlights throughout the day. A replica of a Chinese scholar's garden offers meditative relief, and an annually changing rooftop sculpture garden is an ideal place for a sunset drink overlooking Central Park.

The Metropolitan Museum of Art's imposing entrance.

❻ Follow the path behind the Met, crossing the road to the grim looking building of the **South Gatehouse**. There are information leaflets here for the many joggers who circle the reservoir and to promote the nearby New York Runners Club. This route skirts around a looming obelisk behind the Met, a pinetum and a Great Lawn in this section of **Central Park** (see page 30). Shielded from Fifth Avenue by trees, follow the 'bridle path' around the reservoir, surrounded by the birds and ducks that flock to the great expanse of water.

The Met's Chinese garden offers peaceful relief.

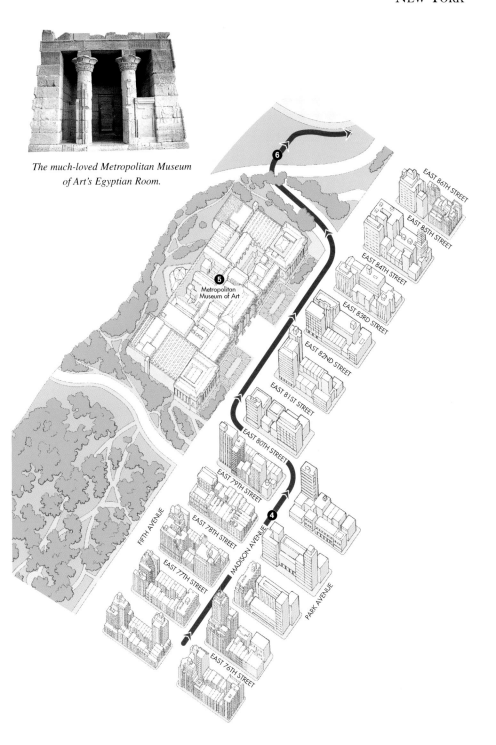

The much-loved Metropolitan Museum of Art's Egyptian Room.

5 Metropolitan Museum of Art

FIFTH AVENUE

MADISON AVENUE

PARK AVENUE

EAST 76TH STREET

EAST 77TH STREET

EAST 78TH STREET

EAST 79TH STREET

EAST 80TH STREET

EAST 81ST STREET

EAST 82ND STREET

EAST 83RD STREET

EAST 84TH STREET

EAST 85TH STREET

EAST 86TH STREET

❼ Exit the park at Engineer's Gate which brings you to another cluster of museums. The white, shell-like interior of the **Guggenheim Museum** (open daily) provides a 90-ft spiralling walkway for special exhibitions of 19th and 20thC artists. Architect Frank Lloyd Wright designed the still revolutionary central body in the 1950s. When the building was emptied of paintings for renovations in the early 1990s, visitors still came just to see Wright's masterpiece. Divert into the side galleries to see works from the permanent collection by Renoir, Manet, Gaugin, Van Gogh and Picasso. The fifth-floor sculpture terrace has sweeping views of Central Park and a new Robert Mapplethorpe Gallery is devoted to photography. The Guggenheim's other locations include SoHo, Venice, Berlin, and most recently, the highly acclaimed museum in Bilbao.

A Guggenheim exhibit.

❽ The three Hewitt sisters are responsible for one of the world's largest design collections. Originally intended as a resource for designers and architects, the 250,000 exhibits from 6thC BC to the present are now divided into four departments in the eclectic **Cooper-Hewitt National Design Museum** (open daily) at 2 East 91st Street. Very modern, temporary exhibitions are made more striking by the dark, oak-panelled interior of Andrew Carnegie's mansion. Carnegie was so devoted to contemporary design he installed the first domestic electric lift here.

❾ In a peaceful, if not remote, stretch of Fifth Avenue, the French gothic mansion of the **Jewish Museum** (closed Fri, Sat) at No. 1109 houses an important collection of Jewish art and artefacts from around the world, spanning 4,000 years. There is an interactive Children's Gallery and a reproduction of the interior of an ancient synagogue. Each year specially commissioned shows by contemporary artists draw large crowds.

The Jewish Museum is in an early 20thC mansion.

Cooper-Hewitt National Design Museum.

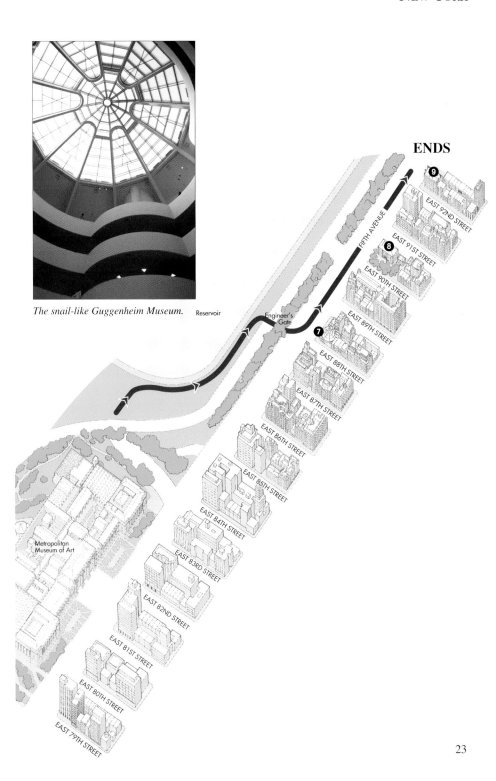

The snail-like Guggenheim Museum.

ENDS

Reservoir

Engineer's Gate

FIFTH AVENUE

EAST 92ND STREET

❾

EAST 91ST STREET

❽

EAST 90TH STREET

EAST 89TH STREET

❼

EAST 88TH STREET

EAST 87TH STREET

EAST 86TH STREET

EAST 85TH STREET

EAST 84TH STREET

Metropolitan
Museum of Art

EAST 83RD STREET

EAST 82ND STREET

EAST 81ST STREET

EAST 80TH STREET

EAST 79TH STREET

A Landscaped Ramble: Central Park

Central Park, the neat parcel of land in the middle of Manhattan has been described as New York's greatest piece of architecture. A walk exploring its most interesting features passes cherry trees, a wisteria pergola and a formal fountain. The route crosses a boat-filled lake to dense woodland and an English flower garden, where a castle terrace leads to the vast American Museum of Natural

Falconer statue near Cherry Hill.

History. Landscaper Frederick Law Olmstead and architect Calvert Vaux worked with 20,000 labourers for 20 years to create a 'specimen of god's handiwork'. Six hundred immigrants living on the swampland were removed and millions of trees planted to transform the 843 acres into the urban Eden which opened in the year 1859.

Detail from archway to Bethesda Fountain.

▶ **STARTS**
West 72nd Street and Central Park West.
Nearest subway: 72nd Street.

■ **ENDS**
West 81st Street and Central Park West.
Nearest subway: 81st Street – Museum of Natural History.

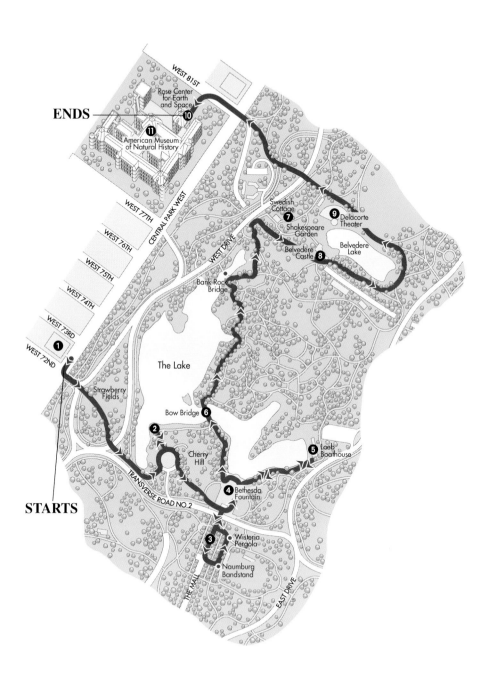

WEST 81ST

Rose Center
for Earth
and Space

ENDS

⑪ ⑩

American Museum
of Natural History

WEST 77TH

CENTRAL PARK WEST

WEST 76TH

WEST 75TH

WEST 74TH

WEST 73RD

①

WEST 72ND

Swedish
Cottage

⑦

Shakespeare
Garden

⑨ Delacorte
    Theater

Belvedere
Lake

Belvedere
Castle ⑧

WEST DRIVE

Bank Rock
Bridge

The Lake

Strawberry
Fields

Bow Bridge ⑥

②

Cherry
Hill

Loeb
Boathouse

⑤

④ Bethesda
    Fountain

TRANSVERSE ROAD NO.2

STARTS

③ Wisteria
   Pergola

Naumburg
Bandstand

THE MALL

EAST DRIVE

❶ When the **Dakota Apartments** were built well over a century ago, they were so far out of the city people joked you might as well move to the remote Dakota territories, and the name stuck. Ex-resident Boris Karloff is said to haunt the corridors of the castle-like building, which was used in the film *Rosemary's Baby*. John Lennon was tragically shot coming home to his apartment here where his widow Yoko Ono still lives. The Dakota overlooks the tear-shaped **Strawberry Fields** in Central Park which was restored to commemorate the former Beatle. Wander past its international peace garden where 161 kinds of plants represent every country in the world from Afghanistan to Zaire.

Central Park buskers.

❸ Step on to the formal promenade of **The Mall** where steps behind the bandshell lead up to a wisteria-draped pergola. A cleverly designed archway under the road gives a dramatic, multi-tiered view through to the fountain, lake and boathouse. Walk under the arch's colourful ceiling tiles, originally made by monks in 12thC France.

Flowers from fans in Strawberry Fields.

❷ Walk around the left arm of **The Lake** where a wooden shelter stands on a tiny cove dedicated to a previous New York major. You can sit in this tranquil spot where the water comes right up to your feet, interrupted only by the occasional rowing boat. Continue over the rocky outcrop of Cherry Hill, where a sweeping view of Bethesda Fountain and the boathouse on the far shore appears.

Cherry Hill shelter.

❹ The biblical account of the miraculous pool of Bethesda was the inspiration for the Victorian **Bethesda Fountain**. The *Angel of the Waters* statue marks the opening of the aqueduct system in 1842, which supplied the city with clean water for the first time. Its sunken terrace is the traditional centrepiece of the park where anti-Vietnam demonstrators used to gather, and it is still a popular place to meet.

*Bethesda
Fountain's Angel
of the Waters.*

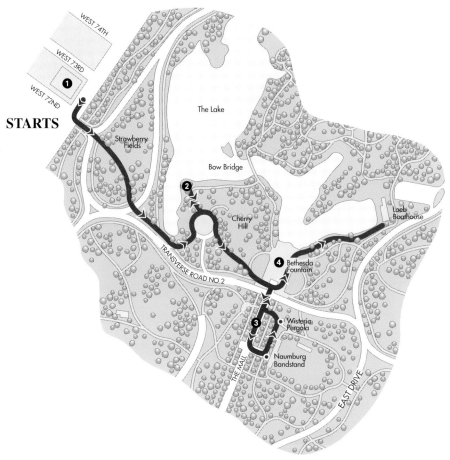

WEST 74TH

WEST 73RD

❶

WEST 72ND

STARTS

The Lake

Strawberry
Fields

Bow Bridge

❷

Cherry
Hill

Loeb
Boathouse

TRANSVERSE ROAD NO.2

❹ Bethesda
Fountain

❸

Wisteria
Pergola

THE MALL

Naumburg
Bandstand

EAST DRIVE

A Landscaped Ramble: Central Park

Gondola rides advertised.

5 Make a short detour around the lake to the **Loeb Boathouse** where there are rowing boats for rent and nightly Venetian gondola rides. Its upmarket restaurant serves lobster salads and tuna steaks on a waterside terrace. A down-to-earth café offers views from a spacious conservatory where you can warm yourself with a hot dog and hot chocolate in front of one of the fires here, or cool down with an ice cream float, depending on the weather.

6 Cross the elegant 60-foot (18-m) cast-iron **Bow Bridge**, designed as a bow to tie together Cherry Hill and The Ramble. The 37-acre tangle of paths dips and climbs through giant boulders and woodland; stick to the water's edge if you don't want to explore. Picnic here next to a stream and you could almost believe you were in a National Park. Some 250 species of birds have been recorded in the park, which is on the Atlantic migration flyway.

A sweeping view of Central Park.

7 The **Swedish Cottage**, complete with gingham curtains, was shipped over from Sweden in 1875. It houses the Marionette Theatre which has occasional puppet shows. Climb the steps to the **Shakespeare Garden** swathed with plants mentioned in his works. A path winds through a rockery of daffodils, ferns, pansies, ivies, primroses and bluebells, studded with half-hidden relevant quotes from his plays. At the summit a gigantic curved scroll acts as a seat.

Music in the air in Central Park.

BUSKER is an old English word for a person who entertains by singing in the street for TIPS

28

This walk has plenty of places to rest.

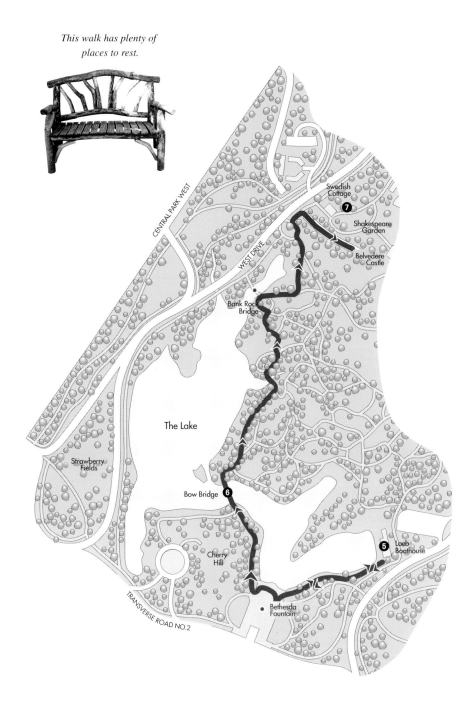

A LANDSCAPED RAMBLE: CENTRAL PARK

❽ Lopsided Victorian **Belvedere Castle** with only one turret is the highest point in the park, giving fine views from the terrace. Inside, a Discovery Chamber has interactive activities, microscopes and brass rubbings for children to learn about the park's varied wildlife, including the bass, carp and turtle in the pond below. The 65-foot (20-m) obelisk rising out of the trees behind was a 3,500-year-old present from Egypt in thanks for America's assistance with the Suez Canal. Cross the western side of the Great Lawn where free concerts have been given by names as diverse as Paul Simon and the Metropolitan Opera.

❾ Overlooking the lake is the amphitheatre of the **Delacorte Theater** (tel. 212 861 7277), the setting each July and August for the free Shakespeare in the Park series. Well-known actors, including Kevin Kline and Denzel Washington, have performed here. Turn up at the box office next to the theatre about an hour before it opens at 1pm to be sure of a ticket for the very popular 8pm performances.

American Museum of Natural History

ENDS

❿ Continue on the path from the theatre across West Drive, back on to Central Park West and down West 81st Street. The startling transparent cube-encased globe of the new **Rose Center for Earth and Space** has been hailed as New York's Louvre pyramid. The entrance is on 81st Street, with access to the adjoining American Museum of Natural History. The most sophisticated technology allows visitors to experience a Cosmic Pathway and virtual-reality Milky Way.

Rose Center for Earth and Space.

There are futuristic installations and interactive exhibits in two halls: Universe and Planet Earth, where children can find out what they would weigh on the sun and watch heart-stopping video footage of a tidal wave. (Open daily.)

Left and Right: The American Museum of Natural History has dinosaurs of all descriptions.

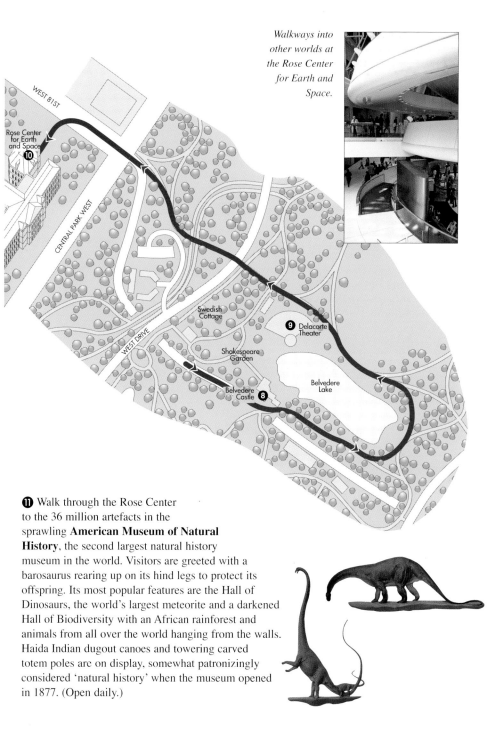

Walkways into other worlds at the Rose Center for Earth and Space.

⓫ Walk through the Rose Center to the 36 million artefacts in the sprawling **American Museum of Natural History**, the second largest natural history museum in the world. Visitors are greeted with a barosaurus rearing up on its hind legs to protect its offspring. Its most popular features are the Hall of Dinosaurs, the world's largest meteorite and a darkened Hall of Biodiversity with an African rainforest and animals from all over the world hanging from the walls. Haida Indian dugout canoes and towering carved totem poles are on display, somewhat patronizingly considered 'natural history' when the museum opened in 1877. (Open daily.)

Art and the Park: From Fifth Avenue to Central Park

The giant mansions of society families in this stretch of Fifth Avenue began to be replaced with expensive boutiques as long as a hundred years ago. The famous thoroughfare is, like the island it bisects, vast, loud and exhilarating. Enjoy its highlights – a world-renowned art museum, a glittering tower and an imposing plaza before diverting to the relative calm of a corner of Central Park. Here rollerbladers, ice-skaters and varied wildlife in the city zoo continue the spectacle.

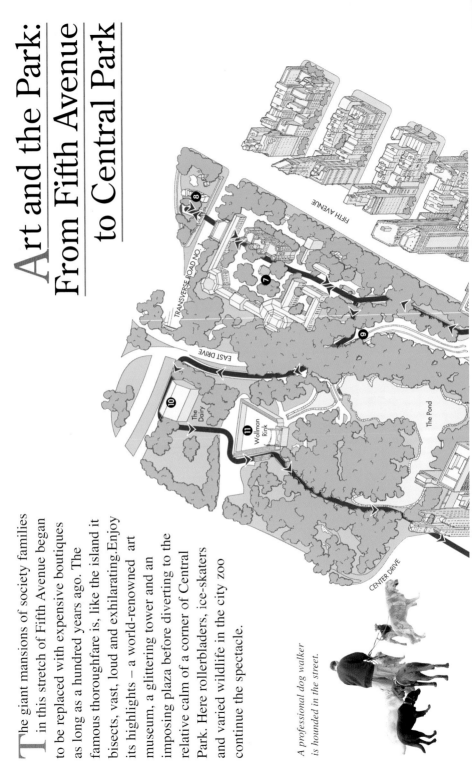

FIFTH AVENUE

TRANSVERSE ROAD NO.

EAST DRIVE

The Dairy

Wollman Rink

The Pond

CENTER DRIVE

A professional dog walker is hounded in the street.

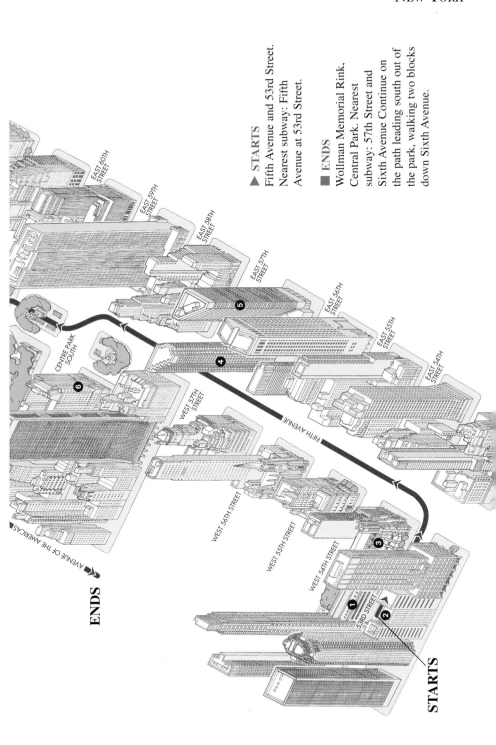

▲ **STARTS**

Fifth Avenue and 53rd Street. Nearest subway: Fifth Avenue at 53rd Street.

■ **ENDS**

Wollman Memorial Rink, Central Park. Nearest subway: 57th Street and Sixth Avenue Continue on the path leading south out of the park, walking two blocks down Sixth Avenue.

EAST 60TH STREET

EAST 59TH STREET

EAST 58TH STREET

EAST 57TH STREET

EAST 56TH STREET

EAST 55TH STREET

EAST 54TH STREET

CENTRE PARK SOUTH

WEST 57TH STREET

FIFTH AVENUE

WEST 57TH STREET

WEST 56TH STREET

WEST 55TH STREET

WEST 54TH STREET

53RD STREET

AVENUE OF THE AMERICAS

ENDS

STARTS

1 Hot dog carts are replaced by pavement jewellery stalls and trees sprouting through the concrete as you near the mammoth **Museum of Modern Art** at 11 West 53rd Street. MoMA (tel. 212 708 9400) houses 100,000 works which trace the history of contemporary art from Van Gogh's Post Impressionist *The Starry Night* to Warhol's *Gold Marilyn Monroe* and beyond. As there is so much to see here, including photography and a sculpture garden, pick up a floor plan and go for your favourites first. Or join one of the intimate guided tours after public hours on Monday nights.

Russian icon in St Thomas' Church.

2 Opposite, the three-storey **American Craft Museum** (tel. 212 956 3535) aims to blur the boundaries between art and craft. The aesthetic nature of contemporary works from exquisite pearl oyster plates to intricate handmade quilts is emphasized in permanent and changing exhibitions. Next door, the **MoMA Design Store** at 44 West 53rd Street sells functional contemporary designs at down-to-earth prices.

3 The 'reserved pews' and the 'no mobile phones during service' plaques announce the popularity of the cathedral-like **St Thomas' church**. Non-worshipping visitors are welcomed with a detailed walking tour leaflet and an invitation to stay as long as they like, and passers-by pop in to kneel in prayer or light a candle to 'Our Lady of Fifth Avenue'. The tiny vine-covered corner on East 53rd Street is a 'pocket park' where trees grow out of the cobblestones, providing a waterfall oasis in the densest part of Manhattan.

4 Step back into the pumping artery of Fifth Avenue, with shops from Gucci to Gap and Godiva Chocolates (see A Shopping Spree, page 122). The **Trump Tower** at No. 72 is businessman Donald Trump's brash vertical piling of shops and eateries. Look inside to see the mirrored, polished pink marble of this over-the-top tower where a waterfall cascades to a ground-floor café. On the fourth floor a small area of trees and seating gives a dizzying view down to Fifth Avenue and up to the offices and apartments on the upper floors.

Candles flicker in honour of 'Our Lady of Fifth Avenue'.

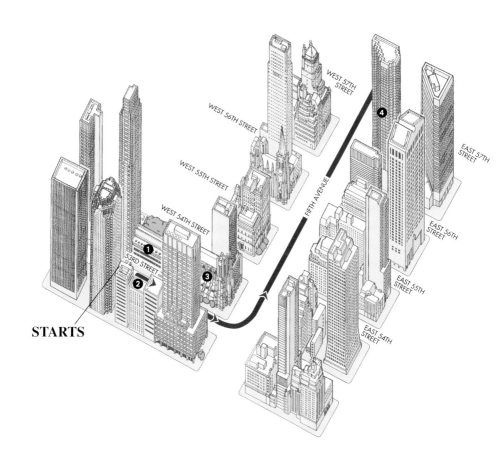

STARTS

Dripping jewellery displays in the Trump Tower.

Art and the Park: From Fifth Avenue to Central Park

Fifth Avenue buildings dwarf the fountain outside the Plaza Hotel.

❼ Central Park Wildlife Center (open 365 days a year; tel. 212 861 6030) has been a feature of this corner of the park since 1864, and to most New Yorkers it is still 'the zoo'. There is a wisteria-terraced café at the entrance, with a brick colonnade garden at its heart. The imaginative design means there are no cages, but 130 species in mostly outdoor climate zones. It is a unique experience to see lumbering polar bears, grooming lakeside Japanese snow monkeys and red pandas padding through bamboo against a backdrop of skyscrapers. Check ahead for times of theatrical penguin and sea lion feeding. The ivy-covered brick **Arsenal** opposite the zoo entrance was built in the 1840s, before the park. It accommodated troops during the Civil War, before housing the American Museum of Natural History between 1869 and 1877. It is now the park headquarters and administration offices for the zoo.

❺ The back of the ground floor leads past a side entrance of the sports emporium **Niketown** (see A Shopping Spree, page 40) and into an airy, high glass-walled atrium. Coffee drinkers can be found gathered around the metal tables amongst the giant bamboo in what has rather hopefully been called 'New York's living room' by one urban planner. Beneath is a photojournalism gallery with free exhibits, films and events organized by the **Freedom Forum**, an international foundation dedicated to free press and free speech. At the time of writing, *Every Four Years* is a thoughtful photographic record, with fascinating video footage, of the presidential campaign trail in America during the 20th century.

❻ The **Grand Army Plaza** on 59th Street is flanked on its western side by the opulent **Plaza Hotel**. Built in the style of a French château, it has been a national landmark since it was built in 1907 for a staggering $12 million. Step inside to see endless gold leaf and ceilings dripping with giant chandeliers, or have an expensive traditional English tea with 'aristocratic' sandwiches and caviar blinis. Horse carriages wait for a fare at the gateway to Central Park (see Museum Mile, page 16), watched over by a statue of a civil war general.

The Plaza hotel is luxurious, some say tasteless.

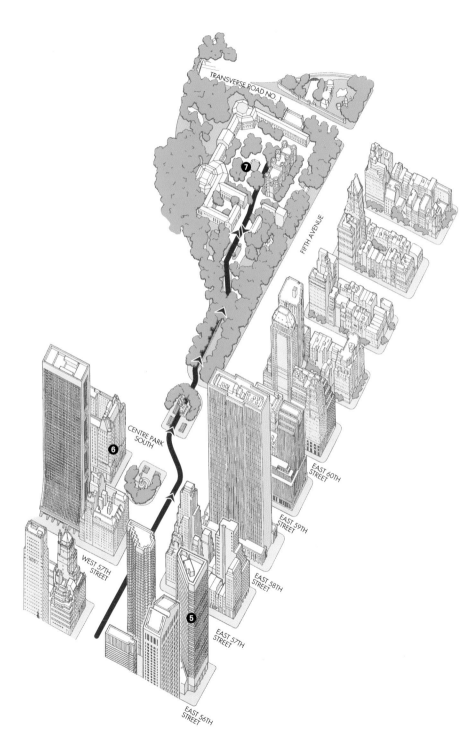

TRANSVERSE ROAD NO. 1

FIFTH AVENUE

❼

CENTRE PARK
SOUTH

❻

EAST 60TH
STREET

EAST 59TH
STREET

EAST 58TH
STREET

WEST 57TH
STREET

EAST 57TH
STREET

❺

EAST 56TH
STREET

37

8 Perched on an arched gate, the whimsical **Delacorte Clock's** bronze dancing animals come to life every half-hour (8am-6pm). A tambourine-playing bear and a penguin on drums, amongst others, circle to nursery rhyme tunes, captivating visitors on their way to the **Tisch Children's Zoo**. Here, children can interact with more domestic animals, pat a Vietnamese pot bellied pig and enter the 'enchanted forest'.

9 Retrace your steps, walking underneath **Inscope Arch**. The good acoustics of the many arches in the park make them popular with buskers from saxophonists to harmonica players. Enterprising performers flock to **Central Park** – especially at weekends when you may come across Chinese head masseurs, palmists, or puppeteers. Follow the path alongside East Drive, turning left at the Dairy.

The Dairy is now the park's visitor centre.

10 The fairytale-like Victorian stone cottage (tel. 212 794 6565) has information about the park's many features and events. It is still called **The Dairy** from the time that cows, along with chicken and peacocks, grazed on meadows here created in 1873 to supply city children with fresh milk. Pass the octagonal hilltop **Chess and Checkers House**, which provides boards and shelters for players, who can borrow pieces from The Dairy.

Players ponder a game at the Chess and Checkers House.

11 Winter ice skating at **Wollman Memorial Rink** –
replaced with roller skating and mini golf in summer –
is particularly magical at Christmas. Come here to rent
skates, or to have a hot chocolate on the sidelines. The
view south of the rink, its skaters dwarfed by the
backdrop of the giant grey towers behind, is a classic
scene. Here, with some distance between you and the
spiralling skyscrapers, you get a real sense of the scale
of the city.

*The ice oasis of
Wollman Memorial Rink.*

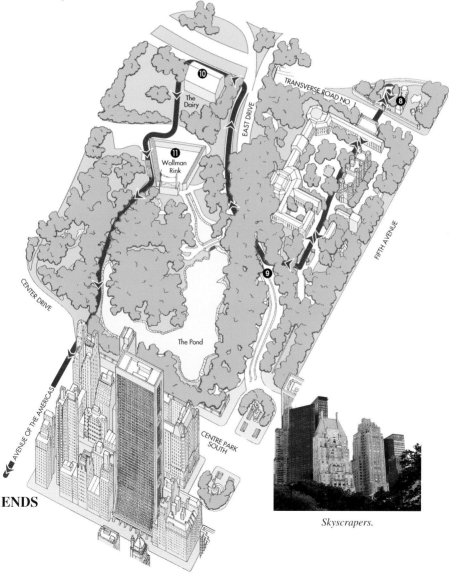

Skyscrapers.

A Shopping Spree: Madison and Fifth Avenues

Many visitors come to New York just to shop, but the sheer scale and variety can be bewildering. This tour around the upper section of Fifth Avenue allows you to blitz the highlights of the undisputed shopping capital of the world in a morning. Here even the department stores specialize, and extravagant window displays are tourist destinations in their own right. Discover the city's historic old-style department stores and the best of the designer boutiques. Although encroaching chains are adding a definite stamp of commerciality, this stretch of shops still screams sophistication. Shopping is taken very seriously here, and there is always a sale on somewhere. Many of the bigger stores never seem to close, but the best time to visit is weekdays mid morning or early afternoon.

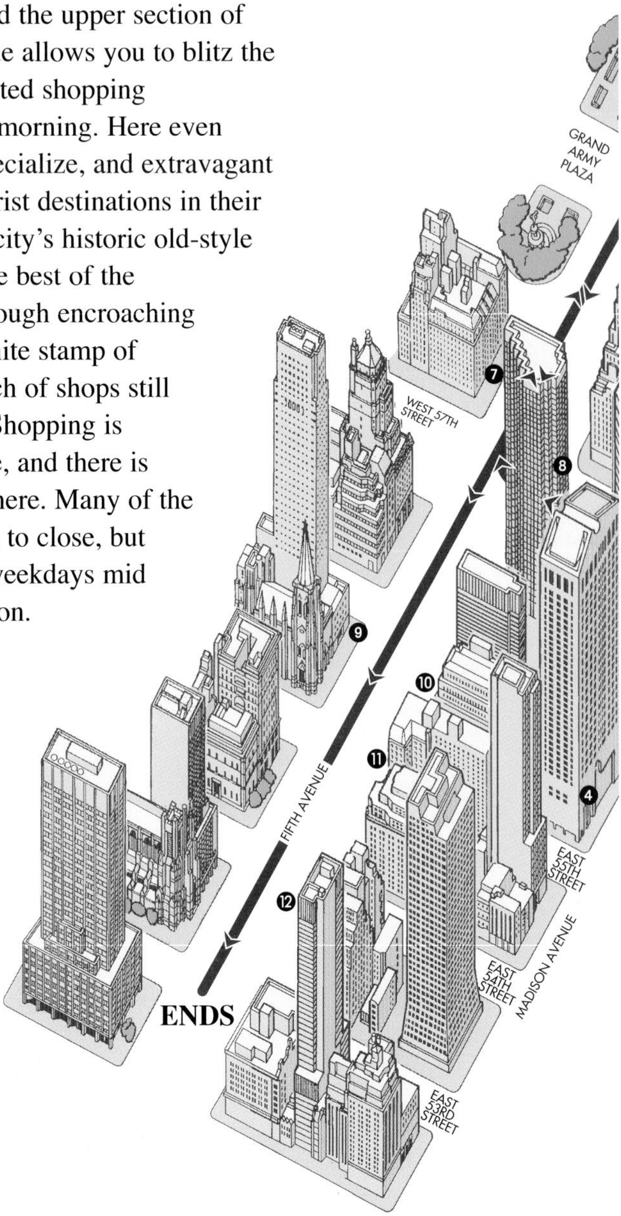

GRAND ARMY PLAZA

WEST 57TH STREET

FIFTH AVENUE

MADISON AVENUE

EAST 55TH STREET

EAST 54TH STREET

EAST 53RD STREET

ENDS

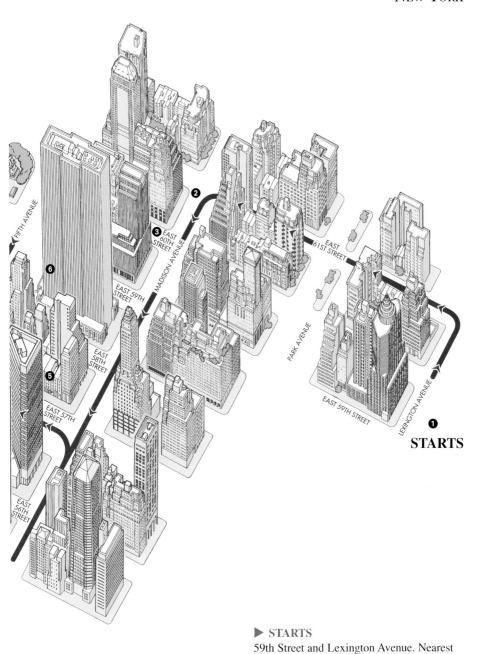

FIFTH AVENUE

2

3 EAST 60TH STREET

6

MADISON AVENUE

EAST 59TH STREET

EAST 61ST STREET

PARK AVENUE

EAST 58TH STREET

5

EAST 57TH STREET

EAST 59TH STREET

LEXINGTON AVENUE

1 STARTS

EAST 56TH STREET

▶ **STARTS**
59th Street and Lexington Avenue. Nearest
subway: 59th Street and Lexington.

■ **ENDS**
Fifth Avenue and 53rd Street. Nearest
subway: Fifth Avenue and 53rd Street.

A Shopping Spree: Madison and Fifth Avenues

1 The Bloomingdale brothers built up the world-famous **Bloomingdale's**, 1000 Third Avenue, from the shop they opened in 1856 selling hooped skirts. Bloomies, as it is affectionately known, is still the grandfather of New York department stores, although it has faded somewhat since its glory days. It has a wide selection of goods, including an enormous footwear

New York is the city of choice.

selection, a shop selling just caviar, and almost every brand-name cosmetic on the ground floor, where a record amount of perfume is sprayed into the air every day.

3 Walk along Madison Avenue, an ultra chic shopping street, to **DKNY** on 60th Street. Even if you are not interested in the latest clothing and accessories from designer Donna Karan, the small, second-floor café is worth a look. Slide on to one of the tree trunk stools, order an organic juice with an anti-stress shot of kava kava and relax to chill-out music and images on a video wall.

Barneys' motto.

2 Turn right on to Lexington Avenue and left along East 61st Street to Madison Avenue, part of an area of exclusive boutiques and shops selling antiques. The *New York Times* declared **Barneys New York**, 660 Madison Avenue, 'so cool and haughty it doesn't need proper punctuation'. Barney Pressman founded the department store by pawning his wife's engagement ring in 1923. Appealing to a stylish, younger crowd, its men's department is one of the most comprehensive in the country and there is a hip home furnishing section. Free alteration is offered on all clothes sold at full price and a bargain-filled warehouse sale is held every March and August.

A department store dedicated to sportswear.

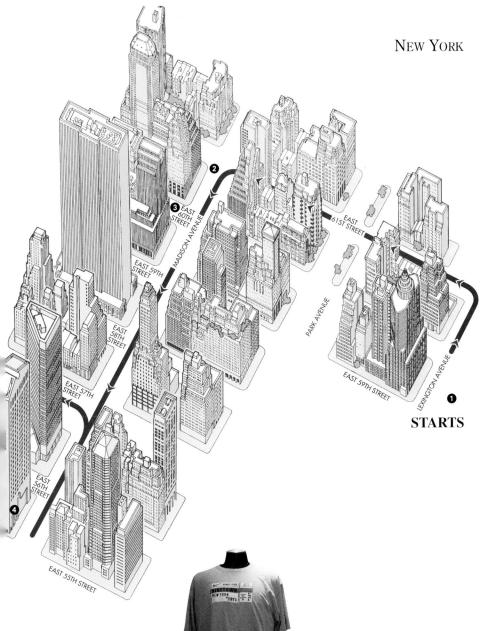

②

③ EAST 60TH STREET

EAST 61ST STREET

EAST 59TH STREET

MADISON AVENUE

PARK AVENUE

EAST 58TH STREET

EAST 57TH STREET

EAST 59TH STREET

LEXINGTON AVENUE

①

STARTS

EAST 56TH STREET

④

EAST 55TH STREET

④ The pink granite Sony Building at 550 Madison Avenue, with its distinctive 'Chippendale' top, houses **SonyStyle** which sells two storeys of toys for grown-ups, including state-of-the-art video and audio equipment. The shop is beneath the headquarters of the electronics giant which owns the

Fanatics of fashion and fitness flock to Niketown.

adjoining public plaza. Next door, **Niketown** at 6 East 57th Street is strictly for sportswear. Most people come to look at the more than 1,000 styles of footwear at this chain, whose branches are sprouting globally. It can be difficult to orientate yourself around the many floors, and the often unhelpful staff don't make it any easier.

43

The Hermès shop was once a townhouse.

❺ Hermès at 11 East 57th Street sells classic handbags, silk scarves and plenty of horsey accessories, including saddles that can be ordered in fuchsia pink to match an outfit. **Chanel Boutique** at No. 5 sells the fashion house's cosmetics, brass-buttoned cashmere cardigans and CC-monogrammed shirts.

❻ Indulge your inner or actual child at **F.A.O. Schwarz**, 767 Fifth Avenue. It is worth making this short detour to join the many grown-ups gazing wistfully at storey-high robots, life-sized stuffed buffaloes, and battery-operated vehicles of all descriptions in this 150-year-old toy emporium, which has its own Barbie Salon. Be prepared to queue at holiday times when the crowds can be almost unbearable.

❼ Visit the marble-floored **Bergdorf Goodman** with its crystal chandeliers at 754 Fifth Avenue for all the major European and American designer clothes. The store's commitment to its distinctly upmarket clientele and exclusive lines can make it seem stuffy, but there are good home furnishing and bridal departments here, and Bergdorf Goodman Men is on the opposite side of the street.

❽ The famous jewellers **Tiffany and Co.** at No. 757 has changed little from its opening in 1837, although it has moved from its original Broadway location. Audrey Hepburn was a customer in Truman Capote's *Breakfast at Tiffany's*. Paloma Picasso is one of their celebrity clients today. It is surprisingly unintimidating and easy to browse here. A pearl necklace packaged in one of the signature duck-egg blue boxes can be had for as little as 200 dollars. Other goods, such as silverware, traditional stationery and china are also on sale.

TIFFANY & CO.

From robot to pedal power at F.A.O. Schwarz.

Discreet doorway of Bergdorf Goodman.

GRAND
ARMY
PLAZA

FIFTH AVENUE

6

EAST 59TH
STREET

7

WEST 57TH
STREET

8

EAST
58TH
STREET

5

MADISON AVENUE

EAST 57TH
STREET

*A highly
prized
Tiffany and
Co. bag.*

TIFFANY & CO

45

9 A man pushing '17thC icons' and 'Russian imperial-style eggs' from 'Russian World' can often be seen handing out his leaflets on this part of Fifth Avenue. 'Bargain' designer clothes stores are often promoted this way, with their so-called 'closing down' sales which invariably last year-round. **Henri Bendel** at No. 714 is a department store just for women, which might explain why it feels so much like a sanctuary. It is easy to feel so relaxed you start believing the helpful assistants are your friends. A sweeping staircase links the floors of designer clothes in this intimate shop modelled on a townhouse. The French-style balcony restaurant has comfortable, candy-striped chairs to sink into.

Chic Henri Bendel display.

10 There are Tinkerbell outfits for three-year-olds, mountains of Winnie the Poohs and Mickey Mouse crockery in the **Disney Store** at No. 711. Twinkling lights and big screen videos assault the senses on

The Disney store is full of characters.

three floors. The **Warner Bros. Studio Store** at 1 East 57th Street has Bugs Bunny Statues of Liberty, Tweetie Pie nightdresses and Nintendo games.

11 It is easy to miss **Takashimaya** at 693 Fifth Avenue, between 54th and 55th Streets. The discreet entrance and doorman of this very Zen Japanese department store make it look more like an apartment building. Wander among displays of exotic flowers and restorative deep-sea water in pretty colours on the ground floor. Downstairs enjoy green tea and cookies in a stone-coloured interior, soothed by the hushed service and low lighting.

Takashimaya.

12 For those whose favourite part of any museum is its shop, **The Museum Company** at No. 673 is a two-storey treasure trove. Its collection of items from 200 museum shops around the world includes reproduction exhibits, modern art playing cards, unusual toys and jewellery.

An aerial view of
Henri Bendel.

The Museum
Company sells
global
idiosyncrasies.

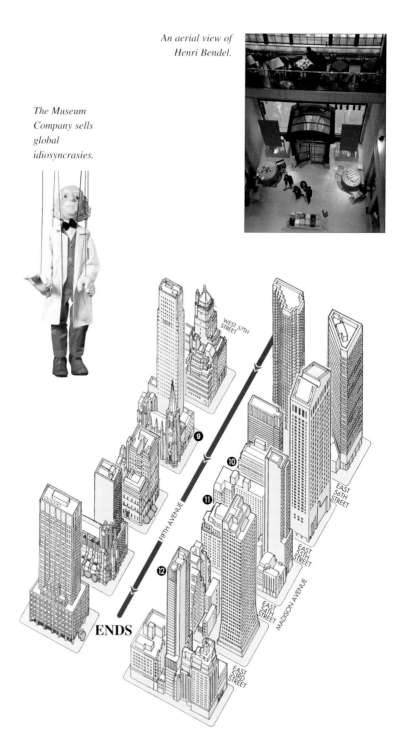

ENDS

West Side Story: From the Lincoln Center to Carnegie Hall

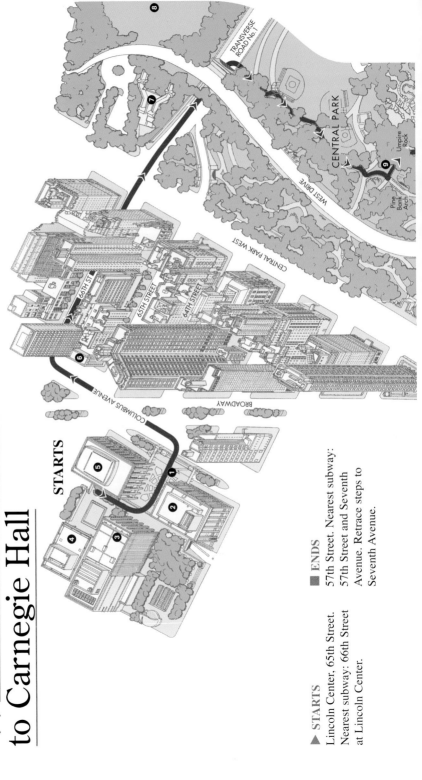

▲ STARTS

Lincoln Center, 65th Street. Nearest subway: 66th Street at Lincoln Center.

■ ENDS

57th Street. Nearest subway: 57th Street and Seventh Avenue. Retrace steps to Seventh Avenue.

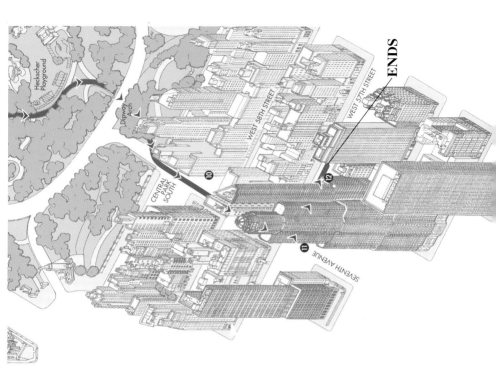

This tour with a musical theme begins with an exploration of the Lincoln Center for the Performing Arts, where every year five million people come to see the world-class performances of ballet, jazz and opera. The run-down tenements which were the setting for Leonard Bernstein's 1950s musical *West Side Story* were razed to make room for the Lincoln Center. Some 1,600 inhabitants were relocated, and this part of the Upper West Side, with its exclusive apartments, is now home to many celebrities such as Jerry Seinfeld. Bernstein had a key role in setting up the 16-acre centre which is America's first and largest performing arts complex. The second section of the walk cuts through Central Park, ending at another superlative music venue, Carnegie Hall, before winding up at the opulent Russian Tea Room for blinis and celebrity spotting.

49

West Side Story: From the Lincoln Center to Carnegie Hall

❶ The central plaza's black marble waterfall designed by Philip Johnson is the focus for the varied performance spaces of the **Lincoln Center**. Henry Moore's *Reclining Figure* in the reflecting pool and a 14-foot (4-m) spider-like *Le Guichet* in front of the New York Public Library for the Performing Arts break up what many argue are the too severely geometric lines of the buildings. During the summer free concerts in the Guggenheim Bandshell in Damrosch Park are given. In August the Out-of-Doors Festival is a highlight of the centre's calendar. During the day, one-hour tours of the Lincoln Center (tel. 212 875 5350) are the best way to see the complex.

Sculpture outside New York Library for the Performing Arts.

❸ Next door, the **Metropolitan Opera House** puts on lavish productions for a loyal following happy to pay the high ticket price. Its fascinating backstage tour – where world-class performers like Luciano Pavarotti have rehearsed – justifiably gets heavily booked in advance (tel. 212 769 7028). Look through the building's five elegant arches to see two Marc Chagall murals on the wall (they are covered in the morning to protect them from the sun). The upstairs café is a good spot from which to survey the plaza.

A sign guiding visitors round the Lincoln Center maze.

❷ To the south of the fountain is the **New York State Theater**. The building is home to the highly acclaimed New York City Ballet, sometimes described as 'a little jewel box' because of its pretty gem-like lighting. Giant marble statues match the scale of the huge four-storey foyer. It caters for a much less elite audience than the Met next door, putting on popular, modern operas and even musicals. Its annual *Nutcracker Suite* ballet is a long-standing Christmas tradition.

Left and above: outside Lincoln Center Theater.

50

❹ There are two theatres in the **Lincoln Center Theater** which put on modern, often experimental theatre. Henry Miller's *After the Fall* was the first performance in the 1,000 seat Vivian Beaumont Theatre in 1962. The much more intimate Mitzi E. Newhouse Theater has seating for only 280 people.

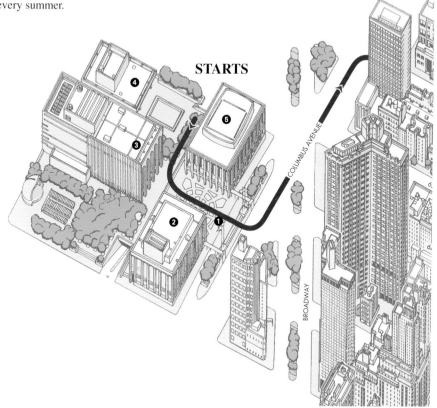

A sculpture outside the Lincoln Center Theater.

❺ **Avery Fisher Hall**, home of the New York Philharmonic, stages some open rehearsals and free concerts. After its opening in 1962 it was plagued with acoustic problems, until the electronics millionaire Avery Fisher funded extensive alterations. The space now ranks with some of the greatest concert halls in the world. The popular Mostly Mozart series is held here every summer.

STARTS

COLUMBUS AVENUE

BROADWAY

6 From the fountain, turn left up busy Columbus Avenue. The unusual cross-shaped **Museum of American Folk Art** celebrates the craftsmanship that goes into everyday items from gravestones to toys. Changing exhibitions, story telling and workshops offer an interesting insight into the country's craft tradition which is often inspired by religion, the family and patriotism. An additional building at 45 West 53rd Street is due to open in 2001 to house permanent exhibits, when the current space will act as a satellite gallery. The Art Deco building at 55 Central Park West on the corner of 66th was used in the film *Ghostbusters*.

Weathered wood carving at Museum of American Folk Art.

The Ghostbusters *building at 55 Central Park West.*

8 Originally designed for military parades, the **Sheep Meadow** was then home for a flock of sheep complete with shepherd. Protests took place here during the sixties. Today cross-country skiers enjoy the 15-acre sweep of green if there is enough snow, while sunbathers cover it on a summer's day.

7 West 66th Street is a nondescript thoroughfare leading to the oasis of Central Park (see page 24). The site of the **Tavern on the Green** restaurant (tel. 212 873 3200) was once shelter for the 200 sheep which grazed on the nearby lawns until 1934. Now accommodating 1,500 diners for rather mediocre meals, it is popular year-round with bus loads of tourists and as a film premiere venue. Visitors come for its fairytale setting with a flower-filled terrace and the glitzy Crystal Room.

A gorilla guards Tavern on the Green.

9 Taking the left fork down the hill, walk up the steps over the rocks ahead to **Pine Bank Arch**. Follow the path ahead of you leading down (not over the arch), keeping the bank of pines to your right. Head towards the upmarket hotel **Essex House** which looms over the park, under the arch where there are tulips in spring.

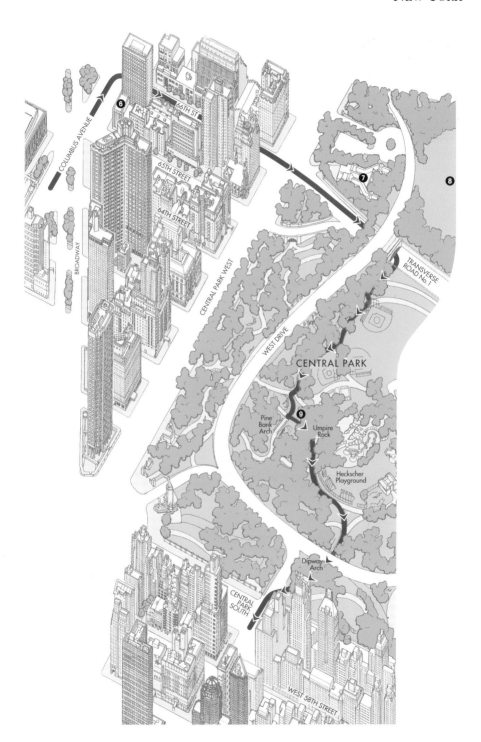

COLUMBUS AVENUE

66TH ST

65TH STREET

64TH STREET

BROADWAY

CENTRAL PARK WEST

WEST DRIVE

TRANSVERSE ROAD No 1

CENTRAL PARK

Pine Bank Arch

Umpire Rock

Heckscher Playground

Dipway Arch

CENTRAL PARK SOUTH

WEST 58TH STREET

Russian delicacies on sale at the Caviar House.

⑩ Follow the traffic-filled Seventh Avenue briefly to the **Caviar House**. It was started by two Russian brothers called Petrossian, who claim to have brought caviar to 1920s Paris, although it had reached the capital by the 1860s. A shop selling smoked salmon and foie gras advises that caviar should be eaten on toast with an ivory or pearl spoon, washed down with vodka. In the restaurant you can indulge in a selection of caviar with cod roe, sturgeon and smoked fish with blinis, but you are better off waiting until you get to the Russian Tea Room (see point 12, this page). At 108 West Fifth Street the intricately carved exterior of Alwyn Court apartments, built in 1907, shows a crowned salamander sitting above the entrance.

⑪ Rejoin the throng in Seventh Avenue to reach **Carnegie Hall** at 154 West 57th Street (tel. 212 247 7800), the world's most prestigious

Carnegie Hall has been a historic landmark for decades.

concert hall. Built in 1891, it still has some of the best acoustics anywhere. The ornate interior constructed in the Italian Renaissance style can be viewed on a tour for visitors. Once home to the New York Philharmonic, a cross-section of famous musicians, including Barry Manilow, has played in this splendid building. See the trowel used to lay the first cornerstone of Carnegie Hall and Toscanini's baton in the quirky adjacent museum. (Closed Wed, open on concert evenings and 11am-4.30pm.) The words "This hall will intertwine itself with the history of our country" from Carnegie's opening speech cover one wall. The museum tells the tale of the 'House that music built' from its opening night with Tchaikovsky as a guest conductor to its renovation in 1986.

Russian Tea Room logo.

⑫ Amongst many others, Michael Douglas and Michael J. Fox have both been spotted eating blinis and caviar in the famous **Russian Tea Room** (tel. 212 265 0947) where Dustin Hoffman met his agent in the film *Tootsie*. For the price of a pot of tea you can while away your time celebrity-spotting in the opulent red and gilt interior.

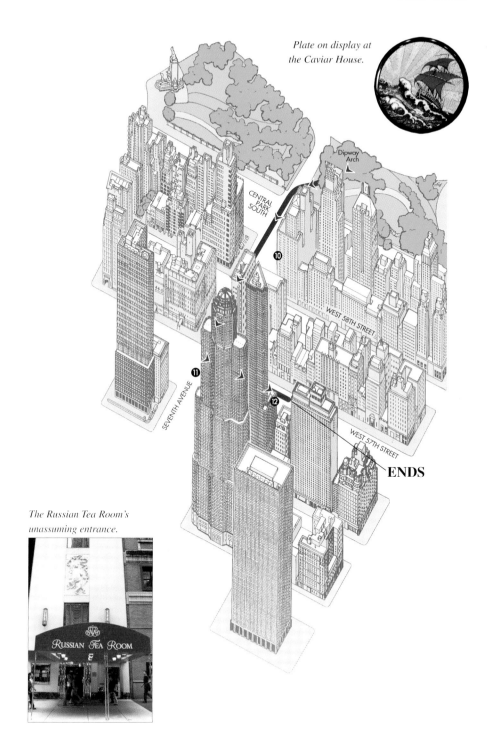

Plate on display at the Caviar House.

Dipway Arch

CENTRAL PARK SOUTH

❿

WEST 58TH STREET

⓫

SEVENTH AVENUE

⓬

WEST 57TH STREET

ENDS

The Russian Tea Room's unassuming entrance.

RUSSIAN TEA ROOM

55

Bright Lights: Around Broadway

New York is a city that glitters. Starting at the dazzling neon corridor of Times Square, embark on a route that guides you to historic theatres hidden in the streets off Broadway. See the over-the-top baroque Lyceum and the Art Deco crown of the Paramount where Sinatra once crooned. Visit the glittering gem displays of Diamond Row and a landmark hotel for literary luminaries. Come at night to experience a Broadway show and the brilliantly lit Rockefeller Center's 1930s-style dinner and dancing at the famous Rainbow Room.

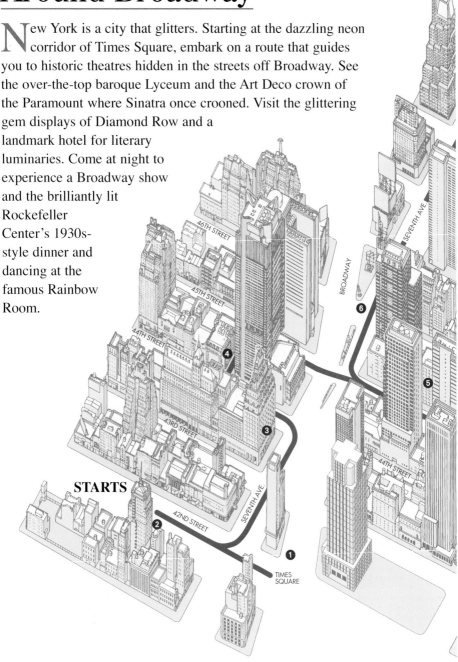

STARTS

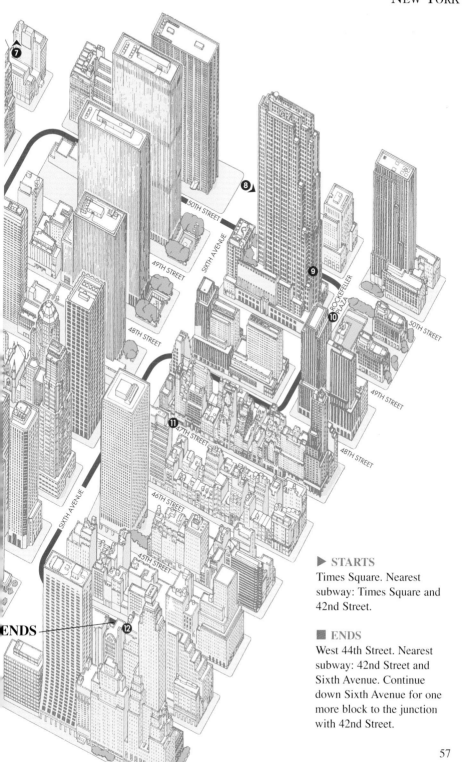

⑦

⑧

50TH STREET

SIXTH AVENUE

49TH STREET

⑨

ROCKEFELLER PLAZA

⑩

50TH STREET

48TH STREET

49TH STREET

⑪ 47TH STREET

48TH STREET

46TH STREET

SIXTH AVENUE

45TH STREET

ENDS **⑫**

▶ **STARTS**

Times Square. Nearest
subway: Times Square and
42nd Street.

■ **ENDS**

West 44th Street. Nearest
subway: 42nd Street and
Sixth Avenue. Continue
down Sixth Avenue for one
more block to the junction
with 42nd Street.

BRIGHT LIGHTS: AROUND BROADWAY

Come to the Cabaret: Broadway's musicals.

① The chaos of neon at **Times Square** announces the heart of the entertainment centre – still often referred to as the 'Crossroads of the World'. As long ago as 1906 Albert Camus described: 'this orgy of violent lights…so much bad taste hardly seems imaginable'. At No. 4 the new 1.6 million-sq.-ft (0.5 million-sq.-m) tower, the **Conde Nast Building** has tiny cells on its surface to capture sunlight and convert it to electricity. The world headquarters for*Vogue*, the*New Yorker* and*Vanity Fair* are here; an indication of how much the area is changing as a result of controversial sanitization. The flea circus, the freak museum and the transvestite bars that made it so colourful have long gone, and the peep shows and the porn shops have all been closed down.

Times Square, one of the most famous intersections in the world.

② The **New Amsterdam Theater** was once the most opulent in the country. The Ziegfeld Follies, Fred Astaire and Bob Hope all performed here. After a period of severe dilapidation, when it looked in danger of closing down, Disney poured in 8,000,000 dollars to have the building restored to its former glory. Nine theatres in this part of West 42nd Street have been renovated and various stages of building work continue in this evolving area.

③ Retrace your steps to Seventh Avenue to the Art Deco landmark of the **Paramount Building** at 1501 Broadway, a wallflower now compared to its heyday. The distinctive crown with a tower, clock and globe still stands but its rooftop observation deck is no longer illuminated and the ground-floor theatre where Frank Sinatra once performed has closed.

④ Walk through the tiny, somewhat shabby **Shubert Alley** where actors once used to line the western wall hoping for a part in a Shubert play. Nos 75-90 have a dedication to 'all those who glorify the theatre and use this short thoroughfare'. A staggering 6,137 performances of*A Chorus Line* were put on at the Shubert Theatre, making it the longest running show on Broadway.

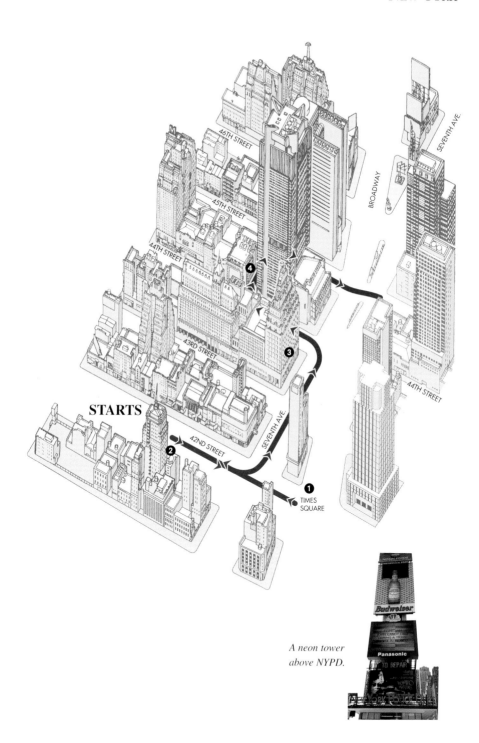

STARTS

46TH STREET

45TH STREET

44TH STREET

43RD STREET

42ND STREET

SEVENTH AVE.

SEVENTH AVE.

BROADWAY

44TH STREET

SEVENTH AVE.

1 TIMES SQUARE

2

3

4

A neon tower above NYPD.

59

5 The **Lyceum** at 149-57 West

Radio City Music Hall.

45th Street is the grandmother of New York theatres and a Beaux-Arts masterpiece. Its faded cream walls display old programmes and photographs from the shows that have played here, including the long-running, popular *Annie Get your Gun*, *Cats* and *Les Misérables*. Walk back to Seventh Avenue and up to **Duffy Square**, also known as Actors' Square, where a statue commemorates George M. Cohen, the actor-producer who wrote the hit musical *Give My Regards to Broadway* in 1904.

6 Pick up theatre tickets and tourist information from the **Times Square Visitor Center** in the disused Embassy Theatre at 1560 Broadway. There are free weekly tours of the neighbourhood from here. In the entrance are photographs of the New Year's Eve celebrations in Times Square. The light-encrusted ball, famously lowered on the stroke of midnight, was covered in crystal triangles, strobes and rotating pyramid mirrors for the Millennium celebrations. It is easy to miss the blackened **Miller Building** which was the 'Show Folks' Shoe Shop' before World War I. Huge billboards of a restaurant chain overshadow the building, with its broken statues of American actresses surrounded by mostly missing gold mosaic. At 1619 Broadway at 49th Street is the **Brill Building**, once the creative hub of Tin Pan Alley which was the centre of the nation's music industry.

7 If you're hungry, make a detour to **Ellen's Stardust Diner** (tel. 212 956 5151), a unique karaoke diner at No. 1650 Broadway. Waiters break into fifties classic songs as they serve 'Be Bop a Lula Bopper' burgers and 'Convertible' sandwiches while a miniature train circles the upper floor.

Fifties kitsch at Ellen's Stardust Diner.

8 At the junction of 50th Street and Sixth Avenue the twin towers of the Life and Chase Manhattan Buildings on either side of the road signal the end of the theatre district. Across the street, the restoration of the **Radio City Music Hall** combines state-of-the-art technology with the original splendour of its Art Deco interior. A one-hour tour takes in the rehearsal hall and great stage.

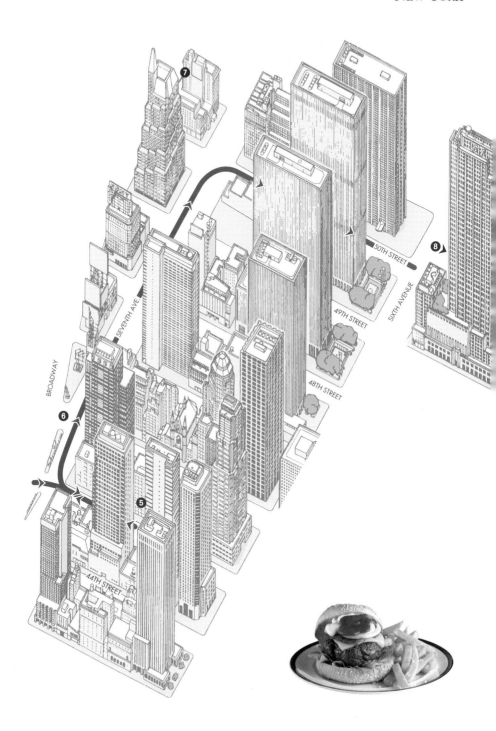

9 Walk up 50th Street, turn right into the pedestrianized **Rockefeller Plaza** and look up at the looming **General Electric Building's** exquisite stone and glass details. The central figure,*Wisdom*, was inspired by a William Blake painting of Jehovah. In the entrance, pick up a leaflet for a self-guided walking tour of the centre which gives details of its extensive indoor and outdoor art programme. It is worth visiting the Art Deco Rainbow Room on the 65th floor for a memorable 1930s-style evening with cocktails, dinner and dancing, and spectacular, almost symmetrical views of the city. See the Empire State standing straight ahead, the Chrysler Building peeking out from behind the Met Life Building, and look right down to the Statue of Liberty. The sunken plaza is the focus of the Rockefeller Center, one of the 20th century's most ambitious urban projects incorporating offices, shops and restaurants which extend to its cavernous lower concourse. In winter this is the site of the famous ice-skating rink which in summer is turned into a popular open-air café.

Rockefeller Center detail.

10 On your right at the corner of 49th Street and Rockefeller Plaza, **NBC** has popular one-hour tours of the studios where its flagship *Today Show* is produced. Opposite, pop in for heart-stopping chocolate crème caramel, dip into the delicious salad bar or grab a strong frothy latte at **Dean and DeLuca**.

11 Continue down unprepossessing 48th Street, turning left on to Avenue of the Americas in this seedier part of town. Two diamonds set on high lamp-posts stand as totems at either end of 47th Street, or **Diamond Row**. Here every shop front seems to be a pawn outlet or jewellery emporium and it's a case of dodging people on the street offering cash for gold and diamonds. The out-of-place Gotham Book Mart at No. 41 sells second-hand literary gems with the motto 'wise men fish here'.

12 Continue down the busy Avenue of the Americas to the hidden jewel of the **Algonquin Hotel** which describes itself as 'an intellectual oasis in the arid philistinism of Broadway'. The intimate lobby just around the corner on 44th Street at No. 59 leads on to the book-stuffed Oak Room where literary lights such as Dorothy Parker

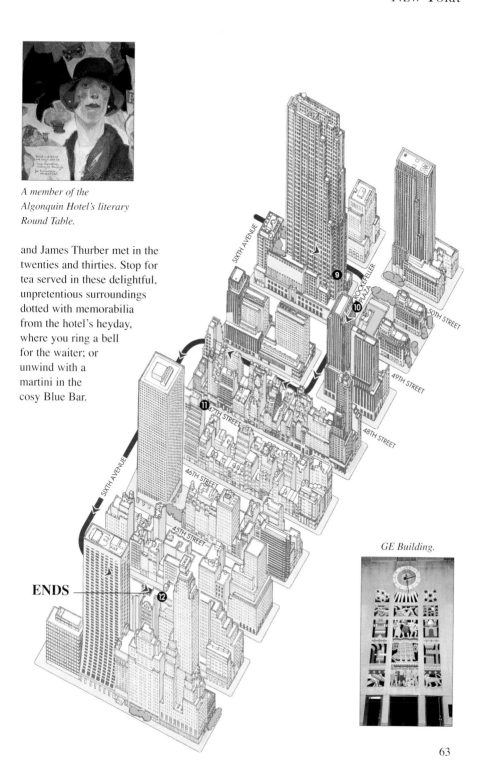

A member of the Algonquin Hotel's literary Round Table.

and James Thurber met in the twenties and thirties. Stop for tea served in these delightful, unpretentious surroundings dotted with memorabilia from the hotel's heyday, where you ring a bell for the waiter; or unwind with a martini in the cosy Blue Bar.

ENDS

GE Building.

63

New York Giants: Around the Empire State Building

▶ **STARTS**

Seventh Avenue and West 34th
Street. Nearest subway: 34th
Street, Penn Street Station,
Seventh Avenue.

■ **ENDS**

Lexington Avenue and East
42nd Street. Nearest subway:
Grand Central 42nd Street
and Lexington Avenue.
Retrace steps along East 42nd
Street for one block to junction
with Park Avenue.

◀ **STARTS**

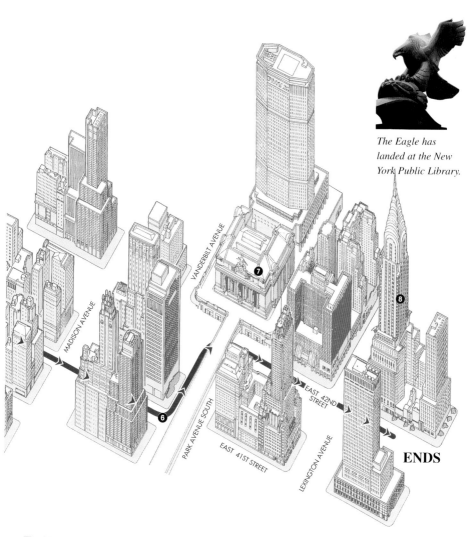

The Eagle has landed at the New York Public Library.

N̲ew York is a city built on a scale like no
other. Hemmed in by water on every side, its
growth has been ever upwards. This walk takes in the
monolith of the Empire State and the shining needle of the
Chrysler which raced to be the world's tallest building in the
1930s. Experience the sheer magnitude of the city's aspirational
buildings, moving from the world's largest department store to one
of its greatest libraries. Lose yourself in Grand Central Terminal,
the 'biggest single room in New York', grander than ever after a
multi-million dollar restoration.

New York Giants: Around the Empire State Building

1 Macy's has its own pet store and fish market, and goods filling a whole block, so no one contests its claim to be 'the world's largest store'. Opened by a whaler in 1857, the red star trademark is taken from his sailor tattoo. Its position in a slightly shabby part of town and the often unhelpful staff means it is more famous for its sponsorship of New York's Thanksgiving Day parade and Fourth of July fireworks than its shopping. During the annual spring flower show, counters are covered with banks of tulips, sprouting orchids and elaborate floral arrangements.

2 Leave Macy's by its Broadway exit. Here tiny, grassless **Herald Square** is dotted with pretty garden chairs and neat flower beds in spring. It is named after the *New York Herald* offices which were here from 1894 to 1921. The clock is all that remains of the building now.

Macy's is a cornerstone of New York culture.

3 It's a short walk up East 34th Street to the **Empire State Building**. Built at an unprecedented rate of four storeys a week as an office block in the 1930s, most of it remained unrented during the Depression and it was soon dubbed 'The Empty State Building'. The hundreds of businesses here now are listed in miniature amongst endless grey and pink marble. Tickets are sold (365 days a year, 9.30am to 11.30pm) in the basement where a board displays the visibility from 0 miles to 'unlimited', which in reality means 80 miles. Lifts shoot up to the observation areas giving an eagle-eye view of the city a quarter of a mile below. The mast which King Kong clung to in the 1933 film transmits televison and radio throughout the city and to other states. At night the top 30 floors change colour according to special events.

Exit on Fifth Avenue and walk up this stretch dotted with mostly uninteresting shops. At No. 424 American flags and green and white striped awnings announce **Lord and Taylor**. The brightly-lit department store that began the tradition of extravagant Christmas window displays is rather past its best.

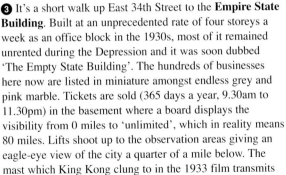

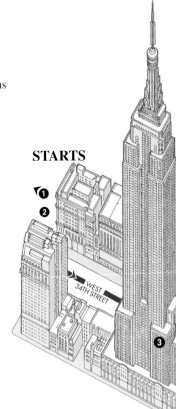

STARTS

WEST 34TH STREET

The 102 floors of the Empire State Building.

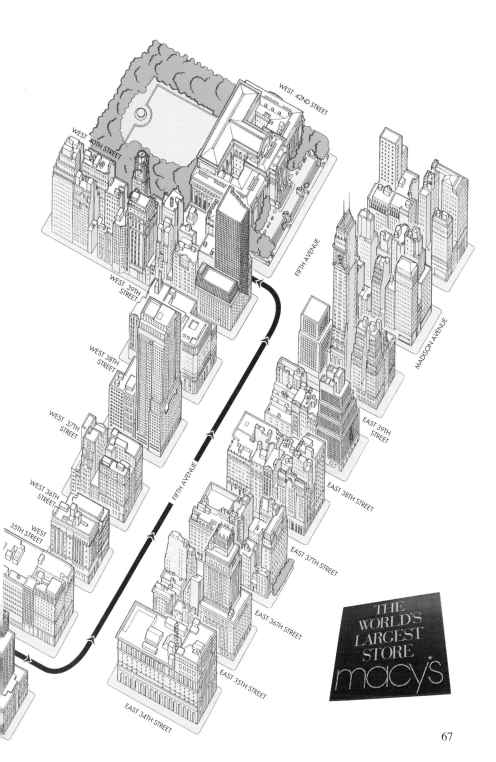

WEST 42ND STREET

WEST 40TH STREET

WEST 39TH STREET

WEST 38TH STREET

WEST 37TH STREET

WEST 36TH STREET

WEST 35TH STREET

EAST 34TH STREET

EAST 35TH STREET

EAST 36TH STREET

EAST 37TH STREET

EAST 38TH STREET

EAST 39TH STREET

FIFTH AVENUE

MADISON AVENUE

THE
WORLD'S
LARGEST
STORE
macy's

4 At the New York Public Library, turn left on to West 40th Street. The striking, Gothic black and gold **American Standard Building** at No. 40 looms over the park, appearing taller than its 21 storeys. Its architect, Raymond Hood, subsequently designed the Rockefeller Center and the Art Deco News Building. Underneath **Bryant Park** three million books are stored in a giant storage area for the library. The park's gravel walkways, neat tree-framed lawn and well-trimmed shrubs give it a Parisian feel. In summer, New Yorkers camp out with picnics for free movies and concerts.

The distinctive black brick American Standard Building.

Gertrude Stein's Buddha-like pose in Bryant Park.

5 Pass behind the library, right on to 42nd Street and right again on to Fifth Avenue to the entrance of the Corinthian-columned, two-city-block marble **New York Public Library**. The building was proclaimed a 'temple of the mind' by the *New York Herald* when it was completed in 1911. Pick up a leaflet for a self-guided tour of the Rose Main Reading Room on the third floor. Light streams through the 15 huge arched windows through which the city's skyscrapers loom. A 15 million dollar renovation of this room completed in 1998 involved replacing hundreds of bulbs in the chandeliers, refinishing the 22-ft (6.5-m)-long tables with their trademark brass reading lamps and wiring them up for 21stC connections. The library, with its 85 branches, is the largest in the world and well used by New Yorkers. Thirty million books and other items are stored here, including treasures such as original Virginia Woolf diaries and a letter from Christopher Columbus describing his journey 'from the Canary Islands to the Indies' in 1493. It is said that the resources in this library enabled the splitting of the atom and invention of the xerox machine. There are free one-hour tours at 11.00am and 2.00pm (tel. 212 930 0501).

The sprawling New York Public Library.

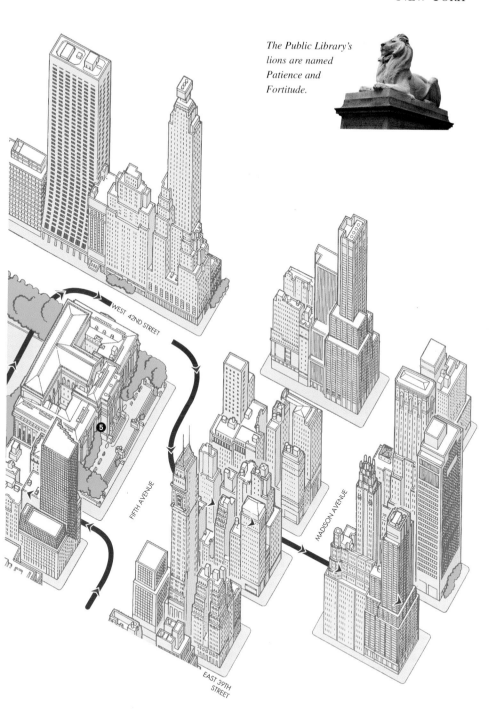

*The Public Library's
lions are named
Patience and
Fortitude.*

WEST 42ND STREET

FIFTH AVENUE

MADISON AVENUE

EAST 39TH
STREET

69

6 Walk down unprepossessing 41st Street. At Park Avenue, the crouching giant of Grand Central Terminal suddenly appears, as if belching cars from its mouth. **Pershing Square** (tel. 212 286 9600) at 90 East 42nd Street occupies a once derelict site which is essentially a traffic island. In an architectural feat echoing its neighbour, it is a wonderfully tranquil restaurant whose green ceiling mimics the viaduct above. A straightforward, expensive menu is served in cosy red leather booths and there is also a bar and coffee bar.

Michael Jordan's Steak House in an unusually quiet moment.

Subdued lighting in Grand Central Terminal.

from outside our solar system. Illuminated numbers mark the discreet doorways to the tracks, hiding the noise and grime of the trains. On the western balcony **Michael Jordan's Steak House** (tel. 212 655 2300) has expensive exquisite traditional food, including lobster, steak and macaroni cheese. For the best vantage point have a martini in the attached bar.

The **Oyster Bar** (tel. 212 754 9494) sits in the cavernous arches on the lower level offering caviar sandwiches, 30 kinds of oysters, and a plethora of fish and seafood from clam chowder to bouillabaisse. There is said to be a whispering gallery in the hallway just outside. Pizza slices, gourmet fish and chips, and kosher sushi are all on sale in the basement food hall. Waiting travellers doze in a circle of deep armchairs at 'Drink City' where the only noise seems to come from the music of the lively Mexican restaurant.

8 The **Chrysler Building**, at 405 Lexington Avenue, is everybody's favourite skyscraper. Its beautifully wrought stainless steel gargoyles and spire form an elegant Art Deco crown which is a key part of the Manhattan skyline. Built for Walter P. Chrysler, the automobile magnate, it was, at 1,048 ft (319.5m), the tallest building in the world for a short time.

7 Despite the 150,000 commuters that rush through **Grand Central Terminal** every day, it remains as serene as a cathedral. Restored over ten years at the cost of 196 million dollars, the softly lit grand hall has a deep turquoise sky of constellations which appear backwards as if seen

A Grand Central Terminal guard.

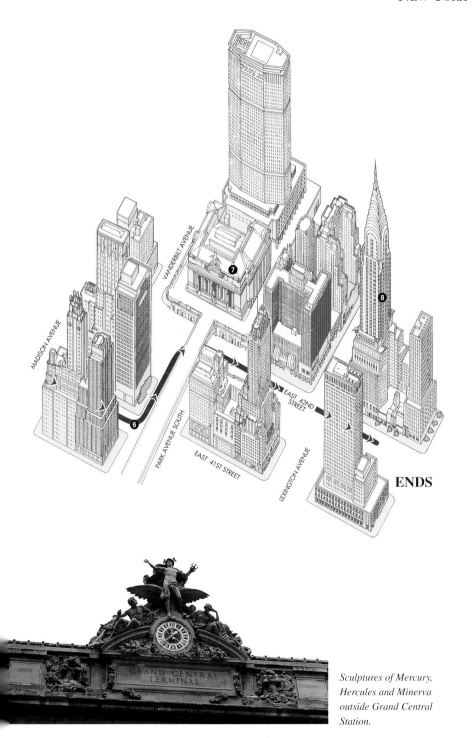

MADISON AVENUE

VANDERBILT AVENUE

7

8

6

PARK AVENUE SOUTH

EAST 41ST STREET

EAST 42ND STREET

LEXINGTON AVENUE

ENDS

Sculptures of Mercury, Hercules and Minerva outside Grand Central Station.

GRAND CENTRAL TERMINAL

Leafy Bohemia:
Greenwich Village

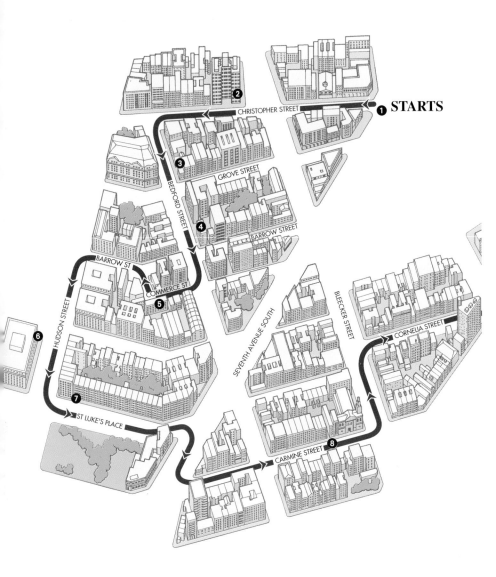

STARTS
CHRISTOPHER STREET
GROVE STREET
BARROW STREET
BEDFORD STREET
BARROW ST
COMMERCE ST
HUDSON STREET
ST LUKE'S PLACE
SEVENTH AVENUE SOUTH
BLEECKER STREET
CORNELIA STREET
CARMINE STREET

A rtists, writers and rebels have always characterized Greenwich Village, where even the random street network defies the grid system. More bankers than beatniks now live in the sought-after apartments here, but the tree-lined streets with their quirky architecture are still full of individuality. This tour of 'the Village' points out literary landmarks, tiny alleys and scenes of riots, stopping off at pavement cafés, hidden restaurants and secret drinking dens. It can be done during the day or early evening, although Washington Square, at its heart, should be avoided at night.

Moustache restaurant dishes up delicious Middle Eastern food.

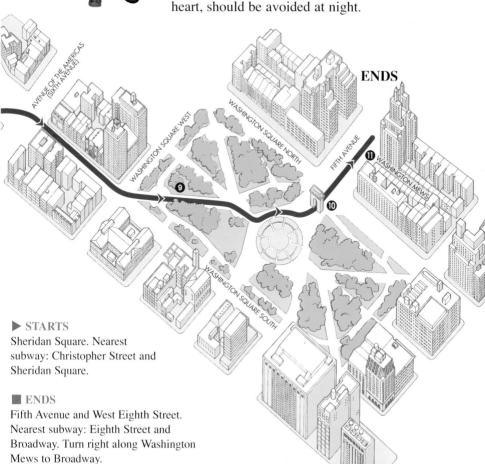

ENDS

▶ **STARTS**
Sheridan Square. Nearest subway: Christopher Street and Sheridan Square.

■ **ENDS**
Fifth Avenue and West Eighth Street. Nearest subway: Eighth Street and Broadway. Turn right along Washington Mews to Broadway.

LEAFY BOHEMIA: GREENWICH VILLAGE

George Segal sculptures in Christopher Park.

❶ Seven streets converge at **Sheridan Square**, once known as the 'mousetrap', confusing even locals. The actual square, slightly to the east of the junction, was the site of rioters refusing to fight in the American Civil War in 1863. A bronze statue of cavalry leader Sheridan stands pompously in **Christopher Park**, but the small triangle of land is best known as a symbol of the gay liberation movement. Well-used benches surround life-like George Segal sculptures of same-sex couples. **The Stonewall Inn** was the site of the Stonewall riots in 1969. Tired of police harassment, the gay customers – many in full drag – successfully fought off police in a routine raid, barricading them inside. The gay Halloween Parade is a flamboyant street festival that takes place in 'the village' every year.

Sheridan statue, Christopher Park.

❷ Wander along **Christopher Street** where gay bars and erotica outlets sit cheek by jowel with shops selling crystals and American Indian dream catchers. Enter **McNultys** at No. 109 just to inhale the aroma from the hessian sacks brimming with Irish cream coffee and lemon tea. Kindly Chinese men serve speciality teas and coffees from this 150-year-old shop which has hand-written lists of gourmet coffees from all over the world.

Endless caffeine at McNultys.

❸ On **Bedford Steet**, notice the unusual house at No. 102. Known as **Twin Peaks**, it was rebuilt in 1926 in this distinctive style as an artistic impetus to the creative occupants. The six houses of **Grove Court** overlook an attractive green courtyard. Although now highly prized residences, when they were built in 1854 the reputation of their inhabitants gave them the name 'Mixed Ale Alley'.

Skinny 75 and a half Bedford Street.

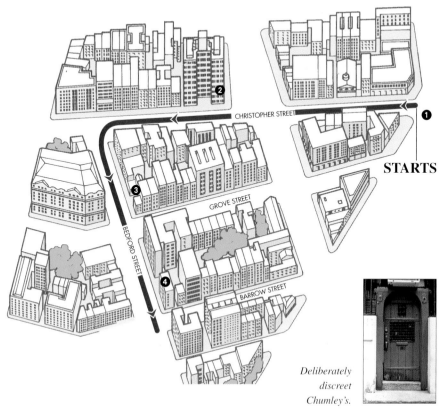

STARTS

Deliberately discreet Chumley's.

❹ Two very different, memorable restaurants are hidden away here. Tiny, friendly **Moustache** at No. 90 (between Barrow and Grove Streets) serves tasty, fresh Middle Eastern dishes, alongside African specialities like ouzi made with chicken, rice and raisins. It doesn't take bookings, but is worth a wait. **Casa** at No. 72 (tel. 212 366 9410) offers Brazilian cuisine as delicious as its South American staff in a cream and dark wood interior that could belong to a turn-of-the-century hacienda. *Fejoda,* the national dish, is a rich beef and black bean casserole served with yucca and okra. It is best washed down with a rum-loaded caipirinha and fresh mint or fresh cashew juice. There is no sign over the

door at **Chumley's** at No. 86 – a remnant from its days as a speakeasy during Prohibition – but a small menu discreetly announces this recommended restaurant. Its steps leading first up and then down were designed to slow down investigating officers. Built on the site of an old blacksmith's, the forges have been made into fireplaces. On the walls are jackets of books from writers such as John Steinbeck, William Faulkner, Norman Mailer, Allen Ginsberg and Jack Kerouac who drank here. **75 and a half Bedford Street**, built in a carriage alley, is only the width of half a house. Pulitzer-Prize winning writer Edna St Vincent Millay lived here from 1892 to 1950. It was also home to John Barrymore and a young Cary Grant.

LEAFY BOHEMIA: GREENWICH VILLAGE

The ever-popular Cherry Lane Theater.

❺ The **Cherry Lane Theater** at 38 Commerce Street began life as a farm silo, eventually becoming a theatre in 1924. The early plays of Edward Albee and Harold Pinter and premieres of Beckett's *Endgame* and *Waiting for Godot* were shown here. Around the bend in the street is Grange Hall, a restored 1930s speakeasy serving American home-farm cooking and popular weekend brunches.

❻ Turn left on to traffic-filled Hudson Street. Three hundred years ago the **Hudson River**, now three blocks west, reached the corner of Hudson and Morton Streets. The river, flanking Manhattan's western side, is named after Henry Hudson, the explorer who came in search of the Northwest Passage in 1609. At the junction, the **Chelsea Garden Center** sells stylish garden furniture and exotic plants and flowers to the sound of water fountains in a jungle of giant palms.

Outdoor accessories at the Chelsea Garden Center.

St Luke's Place.

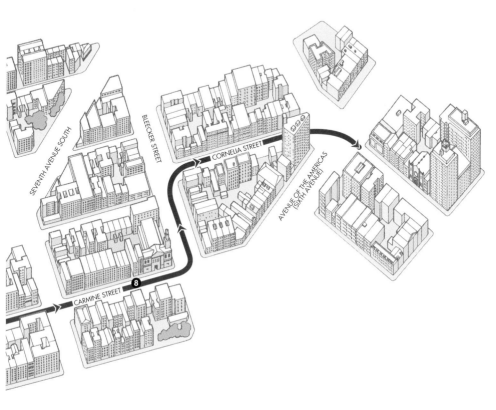

7 On the northern side of **St Luke's Place** look for the 15 Italianate houses dating from the 1850s. Lamps outside No. 6 identify the home of a mayor; in this case much-loved Jimmy Walker who ran the city from 1926 to 1932. No. 10 is the home of the Huxtables in the popular television series, *The Cosby Show*. Grassless **Hudson Park** has ball courts and a children's playground.

Magic Carpet mural.

8 There is weekend belly dancing at the **Magic Carpet** at 54 Carmine Street where traditional Moroccan and Egyptian food is on the menu. A blackboard outside the **Grey Dog's Coffee** at No. 33 offers free coffee to whoever can answer the day's trivia question. Mugs of coffee and homemade cakes are served in this homely café with weathered wooden furniture where pooch pictures line the toilet walls.

9 Zigzag along several dog-leg streets to **Washington Square Park**. Ten thousand bodies were excavated from this site from its previous incarnation as a late 18thC cemetery. There were hangings here until 1819 and an elm used as a gallows still stands in the northwest corner. The park was built on drained marshland, through which Minetta Stream once flowed. A sign on a fountain at 2 Fifth Avenue shows its course before it was diverted. Bob Dylan used to play here, and there is often some kind of performance or poetry reading going on in the central circle surrounded by Japanese pagoda trees. Novelist Henry James lived in a grand Greek revival mansion at No. 18 on the northern side of the square. He wrote *Washington Square* about the close-knit society here, which Edith Wharton who lived at No. 7 described as a 'charmed circle'.

Impromptu acrobatics at Washington Square Park.

Memorial Arch.

Free spirits in Washington Square Park.

10 The marble **Memorial Arch** (1892) leading to Fifth Avenue commemorates Washington's inauguration. One night in 1916 a group of artists scaled it, proclaiming the village 'the free and independent republic of Washington Square, the state of New Bohemia'.

⓫ Gertrude Vanderbilt Whitney, founder of the Whitney Museum, and Edward Hopper once lived in the houses of **Washington Mews** which were originally built as stables. At Fifth Avenue, look back to the park and the Twin Towers of the World Trade Center framed by the Memorial Arch.

Sought after residence in Washington Mews.

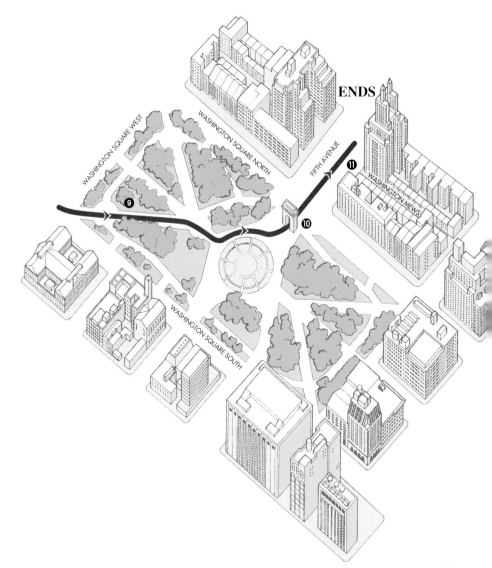

An East Village Evening:
Around
Second
Avenue

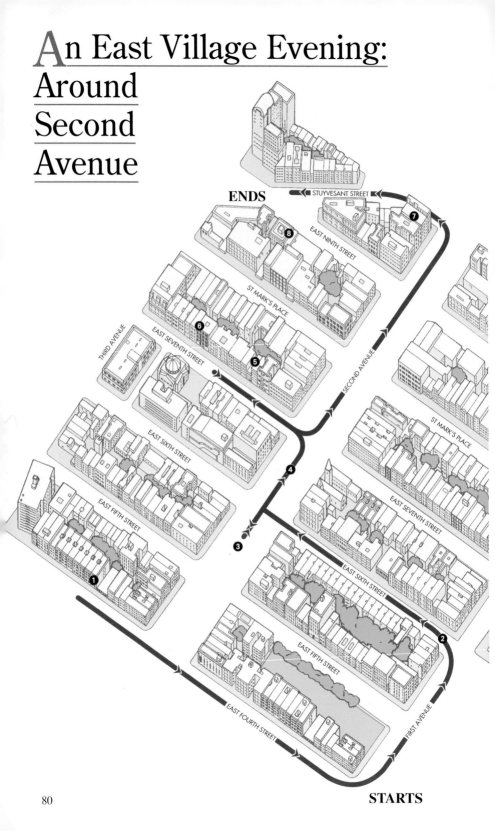

ENDS

STUYVESANT STREET

EAST NINTH STREET

ST MARK'S PLACE

THIRD AVENUE

EAST SEVENTH STREET

EAST SIXTH STREET

EAST FIFTH STREET

SECOND AVENUE

ST MARK'S PLACE

EAST SEVENTH STREET

EAST SIXTH STREET

EAST FIFTH STREET

EAST FOURTH STREET

FIRST AVENUE

STARTS

Discover a unique selection of atmospheric drinking and eating places in one of the most interesting areas of the city. Join

Staff at Decibel, a Japanese-style drinking hole, enjoy a drop of sake.

award-winning writers at KGB, a red den-like bar in the old Communist headquarters and step into a temple of beer, where hundreds of varieties are served by monks in habits. Perch yourself at the bar in a fifties-style Beauty Salon and sip lychee martinis in a speakeasy-style sake bar. Begin at twilight and, if the mood takes you, continue until dawn, stopping for a midnight feast. This bar crawl with a difference is a celebration of New York's varied and exciting nightlife which answers Simone de Beauvoir's question: "What is it about New York that makes sleep useless?" The area is generally safe, although it is best to avoid the streets east of Avenue A at night. Whatever your age, it is law to have some kind of photo ID to drink alcohol, so bring your passport with you.

▶ **STARTS**
East Fourth Street and First Avenue. Nearest subway: Second Avenue and Houston Street. Turn right on to East First Street and left on to First Avenue to East Fourth Street.

■ **ENDS**
East Ninth Street and Third Avenue. Nearest subway: Astor Place and Eighth Street. Turn left down Third Avenue and right at Eighth Street on the next block.

Old-style ale at McSorleys.

The hammer and sickle hangs high at KGB.

❶ The **KGB** at 85 East Fourth Street stands for Kraine Gallery Bar but the abbreviation is fitting for this literary drinking spot in the old Communist Party headquarters. At one time children were warned not to go down this street because, "That's where the commies are." The walls are swathed in red and white hammer-and-sickle flags, old propaganda material and portraits of Lenin. A Russian wolfhound called Ivan wanders around, but the theme isn't taken too far – apart from the offer of a 10,000-dollar all-you-can-drink Five-Year Plan. KGB also happens to be one of New York's most popular literary venues. Prize-winning novelists join the readings here and there are monthly 'round-table' discussions run by a major literary agency.

❷ Walk up lively First Avenue. On the corner of East Sixth Street an **Indian/American grocery** sells a staggering selection of beer from around the world. Pick up a bottle of wheat beer from Sierra Nevada, some cloudy Belgian 'Hoegarden', or a light Mexican 'Sol'. There is black and tan Irish stout, Japanese Sapporo, pumpkin ale and Newcastle Brown in the giant fridges in the back. Any one of them would make an ideal accompaniment to a hot curry at one of the many authentic Indian restaurants lining East Sixth Street between First and Second Avenue in what is unofficially 'Little India'.

❸ Alternatively, make a short detour to the Mexican restaurant **Mary Ann's** on Second Avenue. Luckily, the service is charming and efficient because it gets very busy. The twinkling lanterns, painted wooden wall carvings and pretty tile-topped tables could almost convince you that you were in an Oaxacan courtyard. Sip a perfect frozen margarita and dig into tacos and spicy salsa while you choose from salmon fajitas, chicken dripping in mole sauce and burritos just about any way you want them. Cash only, no credit cards accepted. On the same block, the minimalism of the Tibetan restaurant Lhasa is almost meditative. Calm, intent waiting staff serve New York versions of the traditionally limited national cuisine of which 'momos' are the staple. Try the assorted vegetarian plate of soft crescents of doughy dumplings filled with homemade cheese and chopped zucchini, spinach and bean curd. Religious thankas are the only decoration apart from some photographs of the Dalai Lama, and there are leaflets about forthcoming meetings with lamas – Tibetan holy men.

Lhasa owner – as unassuming as her restaurant.

82

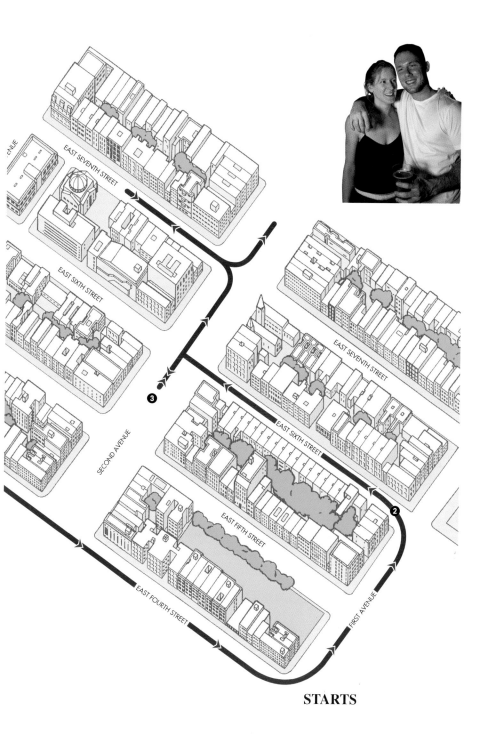

EAST SEVENTH STREET

EAST SIXTH STREET

SECOND AVENUE

❸

EAST SEVENTH STREET

EAST SIXTH STREET

EAST FIFTH STREET

❷

EAST FOURTH STREET

FIRST AVENUE

STARTS

4 The block of Second Avenue between East Sixth and Seventh Streets is a fast-food strip lined with delicious take-aways. You might want to return for a snack here later as most of these places don't close until the early hours and some never do. A **hole in the wall** serves Belgian fries coated with combinations like garlic mayo or honey Dijon mustard. Brightly lit **Cinderella** towards St Mark's Place doles out falafels dripping with tahini, bulging chicken kebabs with yoghurt and Turkish coffee or mint tea to a constant stream of customers. At **San Loco** (No. 124; tel. 212 260 7940) on the other side of the street pick up a deliciously soft floury bean and cheese burrito or a crispy beef taco with jalapeño peppers. The 24-hour bagel place next door is basic but has seating for customers to munch a muffin or a sandwich.

Burp Castle's 'monk' orders silence.

5 Take a delightful detour to **Burp Castle** at 41 East Seventh Street. The 'monastery' where 'brewist' monks serve beer in silence is in fact a bar, but rumours to the contrary are testament to convincing surroundings. Shuffling bearded Ukrainians in hooded habits catch customers with their smiling eyes in performances Robert de Niro would be proud of. The place is loyal to the 900-year tradition of the beer-brewing Belgian Trappist monks, offering a four-page booklet of beers from a dangerous 'Lucifer' to a fruity 'raspberry blonde'. A tiny tongue-in-cheek sign requests 'No talking aloud'. There are murals of monks enjoying beer in heaven in this oak-panelled candlelit room filled with the sounds of Gregorian chants.

McSorley's barman is as traditional as the beer.

6 McSorleys Old Ale House (No. 15; tel. 212 473 9148) was established back in 1854. Stop for a mug of sweet home-brewed ale in this historic, if rather beery, watering hole with sawdust-strewn floor and posters on the walls yellowed by 150 years of tobacco smoke.

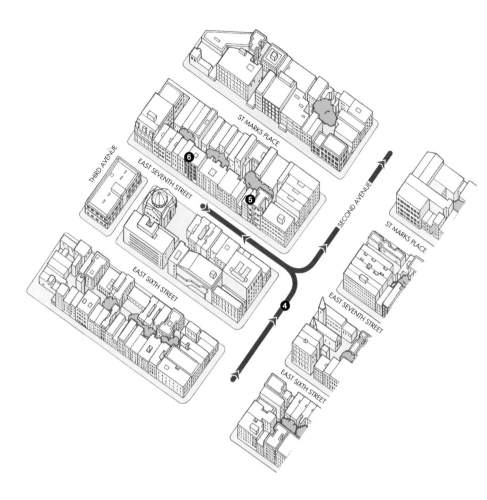

Dipping chips Belgian style at Pommes Frites.

85

7 Don't miss **Decibel**, a small but perfectly formed basement sake bar at 240 East Ninth Street (tel. 212 979 2733). Ring the intercom to enter the den-like, Zen-like interior that feels like a speakeasy. A hot sake works magic on a cold day, but the lychee martinis have to be tried to be believed. There is the whole range of sushi and sashimi on the menu as well as exquisite Japanese pancakes.

Drinks are strictly Japanese at Decibel.

If you still have the stamina make your way up to the fifties-style **Beauty Bar** at 231 East 14th Street between Second and Third Avenues (off map). Sit under original chrome driers and lounge on the laid-back barbers' chairs. Plastic flowers, ice cream-coloured hairdriers and granny-style colognes and potions lined up behind the bar are all part of the cool kitsch design. Munch some pretzels at the bar and choose your favourite hair colour from ancient charts on the wall. This bar is only open at night because by day it is a real beauty salon. The owner has another bar called the **Barmacy** at 538 East 14th Street between Avenues A and B (off map). The decor is just as fifties inspired, but based on the pharmacy it used to be.

The Beauty Bar's night-time treatment.

The Beauty Bar DJ.

8 Join a laid-back crowd which gets more lively as the night progresses in **La Paella** at No. 214 (tel. 212 598 4321). Stop for a glass of fruity sangria and a portion of spicy patatas bravas or some juicy olives at this cosy tapas bar. If you want more than a bar snack, there are serious dishes like 'catalana', a thick casserole of chorizo, chicken and roasted red peppers, or grilled octopus sprinkled with paprika.

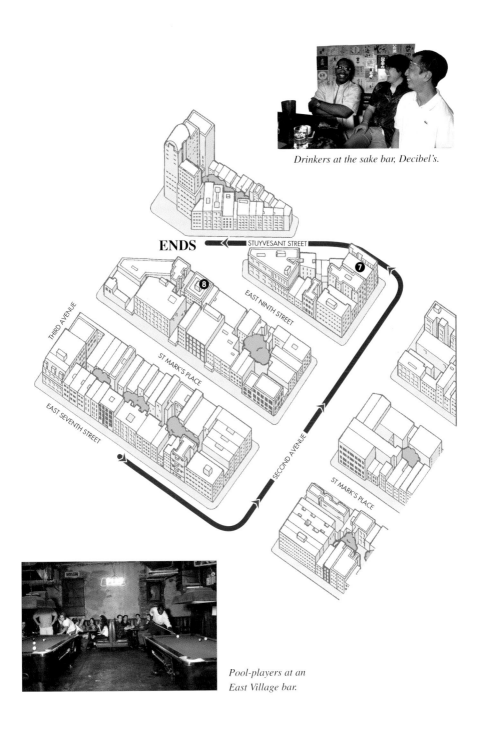

Drinkers at the sake bar, Decibel's.

ENDS STUYVESANT STREET

❼

❽

EAST NINTH STREET

THIRD AVENUE

ST MARK'S PLACE

EAST SEVENTH STREET

SECOND AVENUE

ST MARK'S PLACE

Pool-players at an
East Village bar.

Global Village: Around East Village

This wander through the East Village introduces the area which, more than anywhere else in New York, epitomizes the city's melting pot reputation. From the 1840s Irish, Eastern Europeans, Italians and African Americans migrated here and in the 1960s hippies, writers and artists like Andy Warhol moved in. Although the area is becoming increasingly gentrified, its tenement buildings are still filled with artists and students. This route explores the East Village's churches, tight pockets of vibrant ethnic communities and their deliciously authentic eating places. Stop off at Jewish delis for sugary pastries, or a traditional ale at an Irish saloon. Visit one of the round-the-world food-stops from Italian and Tibetan to Japanese, or Little India's unique enclave of colourful restaurants (see An East Village Evening, page 80).

International newspapers on an East Village news-stand.

Otafuku banner.

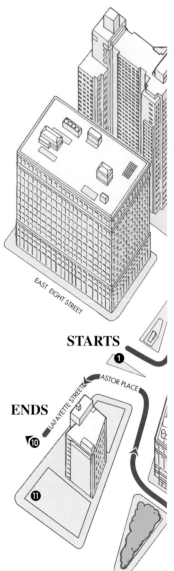

STARTS

ENDS

▶ **STARTS**
Astor Place and Eighth Street.
Nearest subway: Astor Place
and Eighth Street.

■ **ENDS**
Astor Place and Eighth Street.
Nearest subway: Astor Place
and Eighth Street.

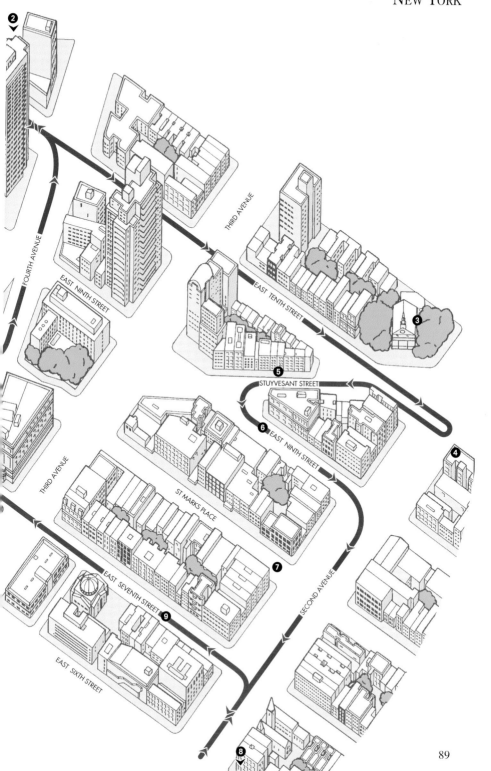

1 An almost permanent group of students crouch around the 15-ft steel cube designed by Bernard Rosenthal, occasionally pushing it to make it perform its one-corner pirouette. Behind, the **Cooper Union** was founded by philanthropist-industrialist, Peter Cooper, to provide free education. Today it is one of the most fiercely competitive design and engineering colleges in the country. Cooper, who built the first American steam locomotive, supplied the rails for the six-storey building's frame, which was the forerunner of the skyscraper. Its Great Hall, inaugurated in 1859 by Mark Twain, was where Abraham Lincoln made his legendary "right is might" speech against slavery.

Alamo, Rosenthal's steel sculpture.

2 The elegant, aptly named **Grace Church** is a dark Gothic masterpiece surrounded by green. It was built on a bend in Broadway (the entrance is here) because a farmer insisted the road skirt his apple orchard. Although in urgent need of restoration, its pretty stained-glass windows, intricate ironwork door and mosaic entrance are still intact. 'A Twenty Minute Tour of Grace Church' leaflet guides visitors to a Titanic memorial stone, and other interesting features. P.T. Barnum arranged for his sideshow performer, midget Tom Thumb to be married here, cheered on by high society and a rowdy congregation. The sexton insisted that "even little people have the right to marry in a big church".

Grace Church window and entrance.

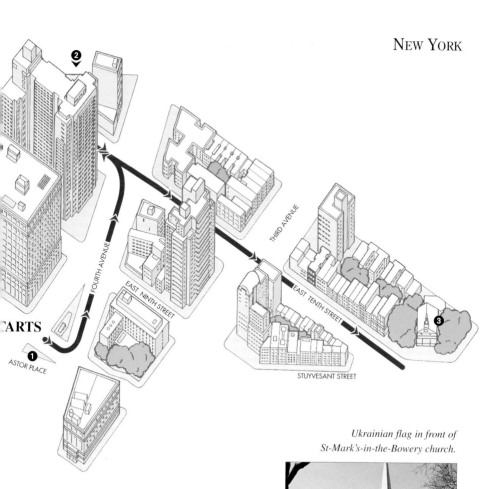

FOURTH AVENUE

THIRD AVENUE

EAST NINTH STREET

EAST TENTH STREET

STUYVESANT STREET

ARTS

❶ ASTOR PLACE

❷

❸

*Ukrainian flag in front of
St-Mark's-in-the-Bowery church.*

❸ Old books, records and clothes spill on to the
street at the start of Tenth Street outside one of the
East Village's many vintage stores. **St-Mark's-in-
the-Bowery Church** (1799) on the corner of Second
Avenue stands on the site of Dutch governor, Peter
Stuyvesant's farm, or 'bouwerie'. The Beat poets
gathered here in the 1950s, and there are still weekly
poetry readings. The Italianate cast iron porch is
often peopled with passers-by sipping a take-out latte
or pressing a mobile phone to their ear. In front, tiny
Abe Lebewohl 'park', filled with tulips in spring, is
dedicated to the Ukrainian owner of the much-loved
Second Avenue Deli across the street. A memorial
here remembers the Ukrainians who lost their lives
in World War II.

Japanese take-away in 'sushi street'.

4 Mohammed Ali, Bob Hope and Joan Rivers have all eaten at the chrome-fronted, neon-lit **Second Avenue Deli** at 156 Second Avenue (tel. 212 677 0606). Hearty Hungarian goulashes, blintzes with cheese, matzo ball soup and other Jewish and Ukrainian delicacies are served to a loyal following. An automat still stands in the entrance, where at one time punters put nickels in a slot to pull out a pastrami sandwich. Across the road, red phone boxes announce the **Telephone Bar**. Here, British staples like lamb with mint sauce and fish and chips are dished up with a wide selection of beers against a backdrop of portraits of the country's kings and queens.

5 Tree-lined Stuyvesant Street was, in the mid-17th century, a private lane forming the entrance to Dutch Governor Pete Stuyvesant's farm, which spread all the way to the East River. The **Stuyvesant-Fish House** at No. 21 was built for the governor's great-great granddaughter and her husband, Nicholas Fish, whose son became governor of New York and Secretary of State. In the early 20th century some of the buildings became brothels. Today, students gather on the steps of the **New York University** building at No. 13.

6 On **East Ninth Street**, Organic Tibetan home cooking is served in the candlelit restaurant **Tsampa**, decorated with Buddhist thankas. Next door, **La Paella** dishes out delicious tapas to a sangria-drinking crowd under a ceiling of dried roses. Essentially, though, this is sushi street. At the Second Avenue end, there are giant bargain take-outs where Japanese diner **Teriyaki Boy** and basement sake bar **Decibel** dish out lychee martinis and sashimi (see An East Village Evening, page 86). Holistic Pet Care on this street provides organic pet food, homeopathy and vitamins for New York's pampered pets.

7 **St Mark's Place** is the East Village's main artery and the stalls hanging over the pavement create a market-like atmosphere, with body piercing, drumming, and young punks on the pavement. The Velvet Underground used to play at No. 23 which is now a community centre. Religious Sex at No. 7 sells extreme fetishwear to clients like Prince and Alice Cooper.

Faces of fashion in St Mark's Place.

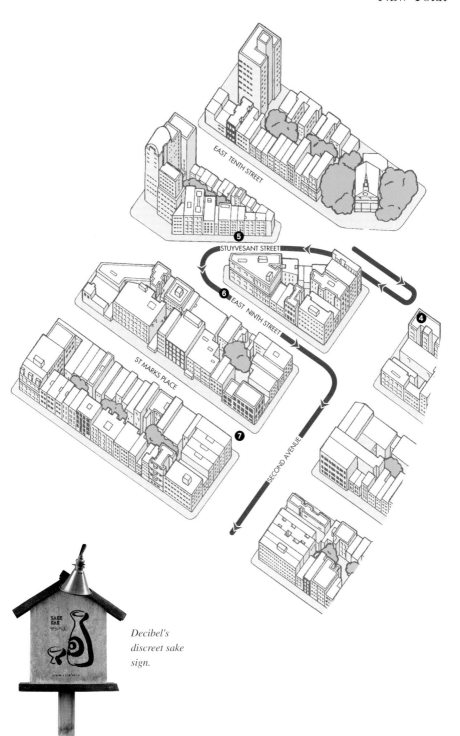

EAST TENTH STREET

STUYVESANT STREET

EAST NINTH STREET

ST MARKS PLACE

SECOND AVENUE

Decibel's discreet sake sign.

Drumming up business in East Sixth Street.

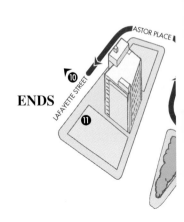

ENDS ⑩ ⑪

ASTOR PLACE

LAFAYETTE STREET

❽ The row of restaurants on the south side of East Sixth Street is known unofficially as **Little India**. The rumour that they are all Bangladeshi-run is irrelevant as most serve up delicious, authentic food at bargain prices. The tiny restaurants compete for customers with ever-brasher displays, so that by the time you reach First Avenue, you have to bow your head to sit down under a heavy swathe of bright fairy lights. Some advertise classical Indian music, bargain express lunches or add Persian and Indonesian dishes to their menu. Others post a waiter to ask "hello, dining?" at the doorway. **Panna II** (tel. 212 598 4610) at 93 First Avenue has wonderfully over-the-top decorations, is cheap, consistent and popular with locals. Although on busy nights don't expect a leisurely meal.

Curry galore in Little India.

❾ Little Ukraine, the area between Seventh and Ninth Streets from First to Third Avenues, is home to 30,000 Ukrainians. The most obvious signs of this compact community are St George's Ukrainian Catholic Church on East Seventh Street and the Ukrainian shop opposite selling dolls, embroidered costumes and decorative Easter eggs known as 'pyansky'. Next door, **McSorley's Old Ale House** (1854) claims to be the oldest in town. Women have only been allowed to drink in the sawdust-strewn surroundings since 1971.

McSorley's Old Ale House.

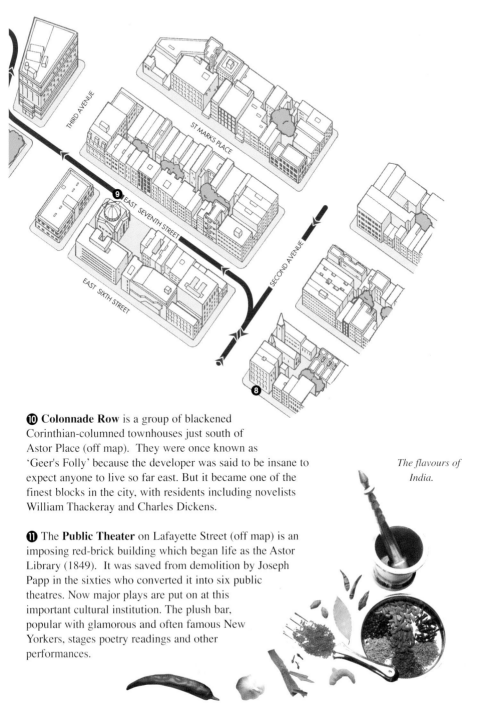

10 Colonnade Row is a group of blackened Corinthian-columned townhouses just south of Astor Place (off map). They were once known as 'Geer's Folly' because the developer was said to be insane to expect anyone to live so far east. But it became one of the finest blocks in the city, with residents including novelists William Thackeray and Charles Dickens.

11 The Public Theater on Lafayette Street (off map) is an imposing red-brick building which began life as the Astor Library (1849). It was saved from demolition by Joseph Papp in the sixties who converted it into six public theatres. Now major plays are put on at this important cultural institution. The plush bar, popular with glamorous and often famous New Yorkers, stages poetry readings and other performances.

The flavours of India.

High Life: SoHo

Follow a trail through SoHo (short for South of Houston Street) which combines the best of shopping, gallery hopping and people watching. This walk zig-zags in and out of the antique stores, fashion boutiques, and highly individual shops of SoHo's compact square mile, pausing at gourmet food stops along the way.

A shopfront's many-breasted sculpture.

Art spills on to the streets of SoHo.

Most artists can no longer afford the rents of its spacious lofts which were, in the 1950s, light-filled warehouses of this down-at-heel area. But the galleries remain; some satellites of the major museums form a miniature Museum Mile, and the distinctive cast-iron fronted buildings are important examples of industrial art in their own right. Avoid Sunday and Monday when most of the museums are closed, and Saturday which is invariably crowded. For information about changing exhibitions, pick up a Gallery Guide free from most museums and galleries. Many SoHo galleries are closed on Mondays and Tuesdays, and from mid July to early September.

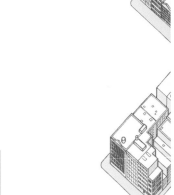

Street art on Prince Street. The artist made the figures on top of the old car. They are old-time construction workers eating lunch.

NEW YORK

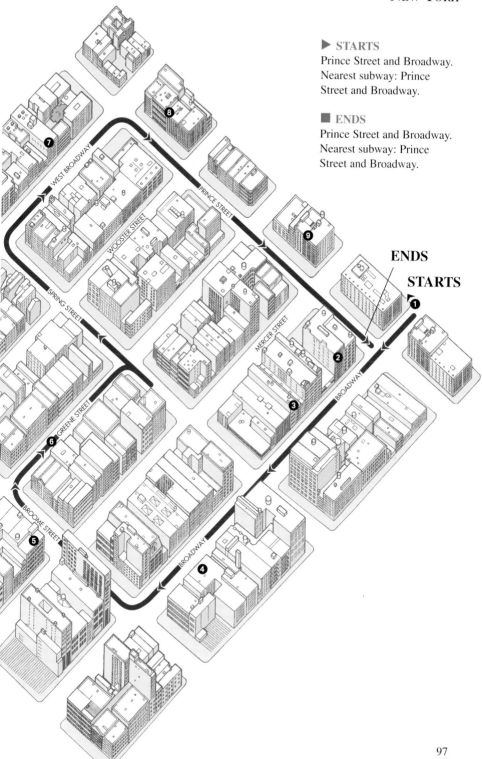

▶ **STARTS**
Prince Street and Broadway.
Nearest subway: Prince
Street and Broadway.

■ **ENDS**
Prince Street and Broadway.
Nearest subway: Prince
Street and Broadway.

ENDS

STARTS

WEST BROADWAY

WOOSTER STREET

PRINCE STREET

SPRING STREET

GREENE STREET

BROADWAY

BROOME STREET

BROADWAY

HIGH LIFE: SoHo

1 Provocative art and cultural exhibitions from new artists are put on by Marcia Tucker, one-time curator of the Whitney, at the **New Museum of Contemporary Art**, 583 Broadway. (Closed Mon, Tues.) The **Museum for African Art** at 593 Broadway (off map) has self-guided tours of changing exhibitions reflecting the art, culture and history of the continent, which often tour nationally and internationally. (Closed Mon.) There is an interesting gift shop, which does not require entrance to the museum. **Guggenheim Museum SoHo**, a satellite of the global giant, opened on the corner of Prince Street in 1992 to high praise. (Closed Mon, Tues.)

Beads, bags and embroidery at the Museum for African Art.

2 Offices of the famous sewing company were housed in the **Singer Building** (1904) at 561 Broadway with its 12 storeys of intricate wrought-iron balconies. It is now home to **Kate's Paperie**, an emporium of 4,000 exotic papers. There is beautifully textured shimmering dragonfly and petal-inlaid paper which customers are encouraged to touch; gifts, stationery, diaries and albums. Opposite, **Dean and DeLuca** began as a simple SoHo sandwich shop and has turned into a New York food Mecca with chains throughout the city. Inhale sacks brimming with aromatic coffee beans from around the world, gaze at mountains of shining Chilean plums and Californian lemons, and drool over the chocolate displays. It is worth joining the inevitable queue for a take-away coffee and a slice of chocolate and nut 'magic cake'.

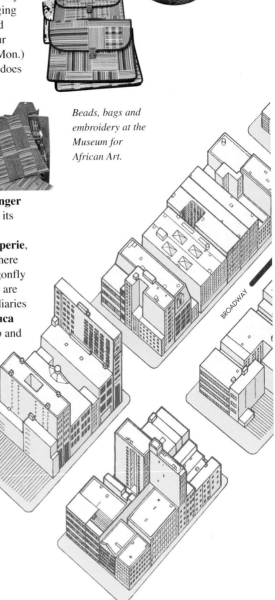

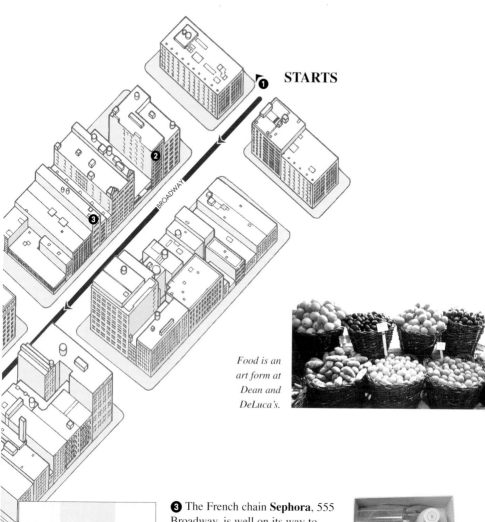

STARTS

Food is an art form at Dean and DeLuca's.

❸ The French chain **Sephora**, 555 Broadway, is well on its way to world domination. It has perfume and cosmetic counters of the kind found in department stores, but there are assistants only at the cash registers. All the big names are here, alongside Sephora's own sleekly packaged brand of edible-smelling products, such as caramel bubble bath and fresh citrus handbag spray. **St Nicholas Hotel** at No. 521 on the corner of Spring Street had a velvet and silk interior, and cost over a million dollars in the 1850s. But only 20 years later it closed its doors to guests when the upmarket hotels all moved uptown.

An exquisite gift set from Sephora.

❹ There are a staggering 7,000 magazines at **Universal News**, from the *Fourth Annual Golf Guide to Las Vegas* to *SWAT: Special Weapons and Tactics for the Prepared*. Its café serving sandwiches and cakes is surrounded by the wall-to-wall magazines. Patrons range from students with time to kill to stylists frantically looking through the latest hair magazines before a fashion shoot. On the corner of Broadway and Broome Street, the cast-iron, Renaissance-inspired **Haughwort Building** (1857) was designed for a prestigious china and glass company which once supplied the White House. The Haughwort was the first building to use the Otis elevator, which made skyscrapers possible.

Above and below: Evolution's Skeleton and staff.

more highly regarded. There are designer shops here such as Helmut Lang, agnès b. and Vivienne Westwood. Turn right on to Spring Street for a short detour to **Evolution** at No. 120 which sells huge-winged luminescent butterflies, bottled sand sharks, racoon penis bones and glinting 360 million-year-old fossil ammonites. The shop, which claims not to stock endangered species, will sell you your very own 100 million-year-old dinosaur tooth from Mexico for $30.00. On the corner of Spring and Wooster Streets, there is a cluster of stalls selling women's fashion, jewellery and bags.

❺ Grab a 'Starving Artist' sandwich and a fresh fruit smoothie, and try to get a seat on one of the benches outside the **Gourmet Garage** at 453 Broome Street. The focus of this deli is on organic produce, rather than the imported delicacies of Dean and DeLuca, but it is no less mouth-watering. There is daily fresh doughy bread filled with chocolate, sesame seeds or olives, every kind of homemade soup from miso to faglio and 15 kinds of gleaming olives.

❻ Turn right on to **Greene Street**. This block has 13 complete cast-iron fronts, which at one time could be ordered from a catalogue, painted, and put on the front of a building for a cheap, stylish appearance. The buildings are individually painted – chocolate brown, blue, cream and grey – with matching fire escapes. The cream-fronted ornate pillars of Nos. 72-76 mark the 'King of Greene Street', but the 'Queen' at Nos. 28-30 is even

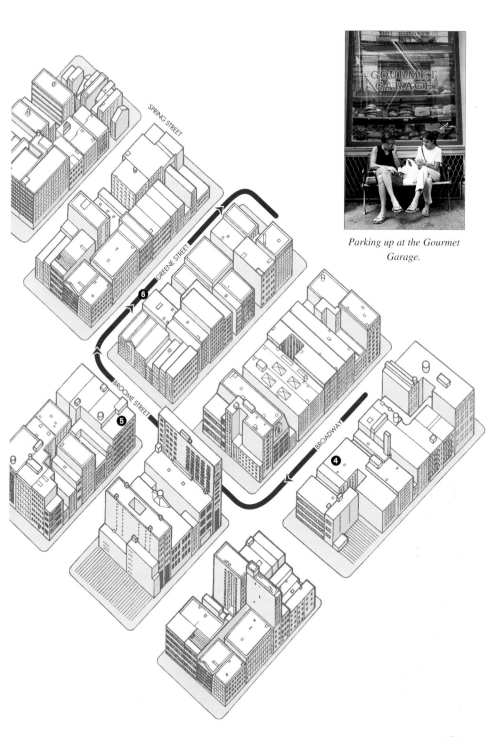

SPRING STREET

GREENE STREET

6

BROOME STREET

5

BROADWAY

4

Parking up at the Gourmet Garage.

❼ Turn right on to busy **West Broadway**. At No. 375 pretty floral sundresses, fringed linen skirts and hand-beaded sandals are some of the prairie-inspired clothes at Anthropologie. 'The Broken Kilometer' is a

Prince Street stall

125-foot (38-m) semi-permanent installation by Walter de Maria at No. 393. It consists of 500 intensely lit, highly polished brass rods seemingly stretching to infinity. The dependable Nancy Hoffman gallery, at No. 429 has been here since the seventies. Opposite, at No. 420, Leo Castelli discovered some big names in the American art world in the sixties and his gallery is one of SoHo's largest. The Sonnabend Gallery on the third floor has some major works by contemporary artists who have included Gilbert and George and Haim Steinbach.

❽ **Prince Street's** stalls sell handcrafted jewellery, art books and the latest film scripts. On the corner of Greene and Prince Streets notice a *trompe-l'oeil* of a cast-iron front, which even shows a window-gazing cat. Pablo Picasso, Georg Baselitz and Agnes Martin are a few of the artists whose work has been exhibited at **Pace Wildenstein** (142 Greene Street), downtown branch of the well-known 57th Street gallery. On the second floor, Sperone Westwater shows established 20thC artists, specializing in work by Italian Neo-Expressionists like Sandro Chia and Francesco Clemente.

❾ Visit the **Mercer Kitchen** at 99 Prince Street (tel. 212 966 5454) for exquisite food, such as oysters, black truffle pizza and roasted black sea bass, in elegant surroundings. The restaurant and leather-sofa'd bar is part of the chic Mercer Hotel. **SoHo Sanctuary's** discreet entrance at 119 Mercer Street leads to a classic SoHo loft that is minimal apart from some positive affirmations around the changing rooms. There are relaxing, restorative aromatherapy massages, a steam room and mud body treatments (tel. 212 334 5550).

Artists chalk up a living on SoHo's pavements.

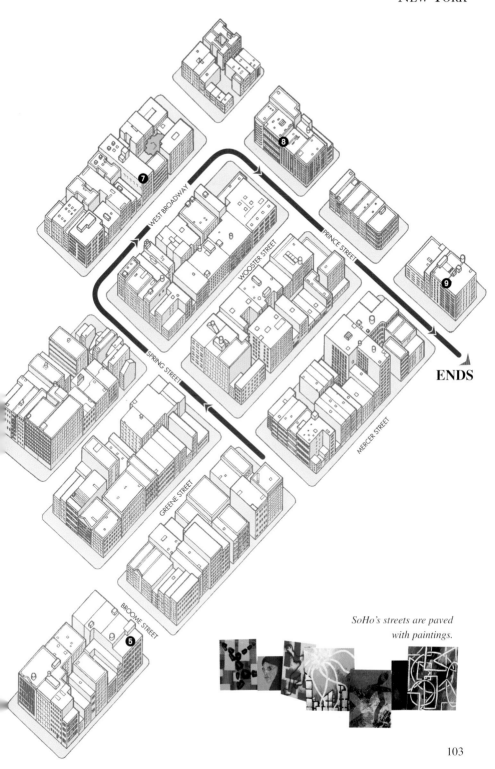

SoHo's streets are paved with paintings.

103

A Gourmet Trail: Little Italy and Chinatown

Soak up the colours and flavours of Little Italy and Chinatown on this eating trail which guides you through narrow crowded streets packed with exotic goods. Sampling delicacies en route is the best way to immerse yourself in these unique corners of New York. Thread your way past street hawkers and markets selling some of the best fish, vegetables and fruit in the city. Eat in one of the 400 restaurants crammed into Chinatown which cover the whole spectrum from Szechuan to Vietnamese in one of the largest Chinese communities in the western world. Stop for doughy filled dumplings, or for coffee and biscotti at New York's first espresso bar. Visit a Chinese ice cream factory, a hundred-year-old Italian cheese shop, and say a prayer at a Buddhist temple.

STARTS

SPRING STREET

BROOME STREET

LAFAYETTE STREET

CENTRE STREET

CENTRE MARKET PLACE

MULBERRY STREET

GRAND STREET

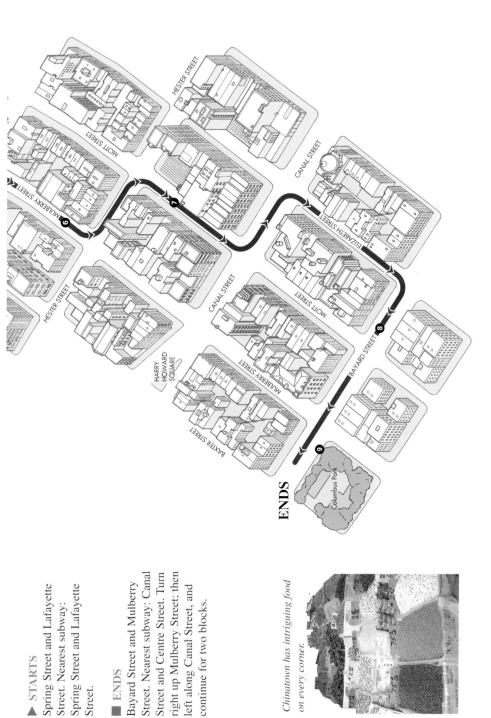

MOTT STREET

HESTER STREET

MULBERRY STREET

HESTER STREET

CANAL STREET

HARRY HOWARD SQUARE

CANAL STREET

MULBERRY STREET

BAXTER STREET

CANAL STREET

ELIZABETH STREET

MOTT STREET

BAYARD STREET

ENDS

Columbus Park

▲ STARTS

Spring Street and Lafayette Street. Nearest subway: Spring Street and Lafayette Street.

■ ENDS

Bayard Street and Mulberry Street. Nearest subway: Canal Street and Centre Street. Turn right up Mulberry Street; then left along Canal Street, and continue for two blocks.

Chinatown has intriguing food on every corner.

A Gourmet Trail: Little Italy and Chinatown

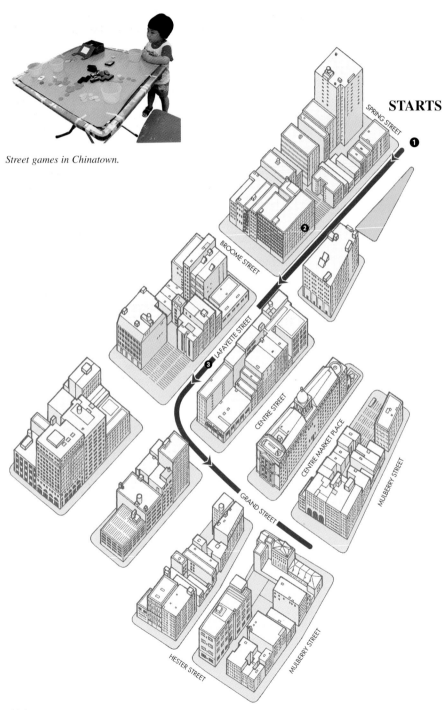

Street games in Chinatown.

STARTS

SPRING STREET

❶

❷

BROOME STREET

LAFAYETTE STREET

❸

CENTRE STREET

CENTRE MARKET PLACE

MULBERRY STREET

GRAND STREET

HESTER STREET

MULBERRY STREET

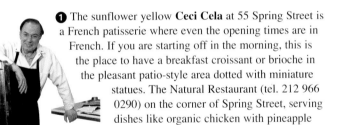

1 The sunflower yellow **Ceci Cela** at 55 Spring Street is a French patisserie where even the opening times are in French. If you are starting off in the morning, this is the place to have a breakfast croissant or brioche in the pleasant patio-style area dotted with miniature statues. The Natural Restaurant (tel. 212 966 0290) on the corner of Spring Street, serving dishes like organic chicken with pineapple mustard glaze and jumbo shrimps with roasted garlic, is popular with locals.

Dom's Italian owner shows off his sausages.

2 Look out for the neon chicken and coffee cup in the window of **Doms** at 202 Lafayette Street. Dom and his brother from Naples pride themselves on the fresh sausages they make daily at this Italian food hall. Take home a string of them or choose from take-out tiramisu, tortellini with pancetta and asparagus, fresh soups, house salads and a full range of antipasti.

3 Chinatown suddenly begins in this part of Lafayette Street. Turn left along Grand Street and step inside the **Phoenix Poultry Market** at No. 159 to see a macabre process in which customers pick a duck or other bird from a cage. It is whisked away by its wings behind a plastic curtain and within seconds a man in an apron delivers the fowl to its new owners in thin red plastic bags. Next door, oysters and shrimps sit in buckets alongside giant bags of fried maw outside a food market. Inside there are Chinese quail eggs and various kinds of uncooked noodles. You might want to try a carton of iced chrysanthemum tea, guava juice, or a can of strong Japanese beer.

The Italian Food Center's olive oil wall.

Kitsch and kimonos at Grand Street's Chinese emporium.

❹ The aroma of fresh pizza dough fills the air in the **Italian Food Center** at No. 186 Grand Street. Go in just to look at the giant jars of spicy sausages in thick red chilli oil, frosted capers, and glistening green gherkins. Pick up a rice ball filled with romano cheese or a soft doughy dumpling layered with spinach and topped with melted mozzarella to eat on the bench outside. Next door at No. 188 a 100-year-old cheese-making shop with a tin ceiling sells over 4,000 pounds of ricotta, smoked mozzarella, marscapone and gorgonzola every week. In the window of the ravioli shop next door at No. 190 are displays of green, white and black squid ink tortellini, and jumbo fluted orange circles of ravioli. Inside the shop, founded in 1920, are strings of spaghetti made on the premises and blocks of fresh parmesan.

❺ Make a short detour to **Ferrara's** at 195 Grand Street which was the city's first espresso bar when it opened in 1892. Take away a bag of almond biscotti, chocolate shells filled with sweet ricotta cream, or an 'Italian pick-me-up' of tiramisu ice cream. Upstairs is a huge wood-panelled seating area with marble floors and waitress service where you can choose from two pages of Italian desserts. Opposite, a Chinese shop sells dried abalone in jars, hundreds of kinds of ginseng,

sliced deer antler, and dried seahorses for flavouring soup. A chaotic **Chinese emporium** at 200 Grand Street has silk purses, kimonos, brightly coloured lanterns and huge decorated thermos flasks.

❻ **Mulberry Street** is the heart of Little Italy. This is the traditional centre of the community which was portrayed so vividly in Martin Scorsese's *Mean Streets*, where every September Italians converge to celebrate the Feast of San Gennaro. Chinatown has grown so rapidly that the Italian quarter is now compressed into a small area around this one street, but there are plenty of good restaurants here serving fantastic pasta and seafood; many with tables outside. At No. 128 Mulberry Street, on the corner with Grand Street, **Foranzo Italian Imports** sells a bizarre collection of dusty Italian goods including football shirts, espresso machines, cookery magazines and papal memorabilia. **Umberto's Clam House** on the corner of Hester Street, where Mafia boss Joey Gallo was famously shot in 1972, still serves seafood to a loyal clientele.

The ravioli shop's fantastic pasta.

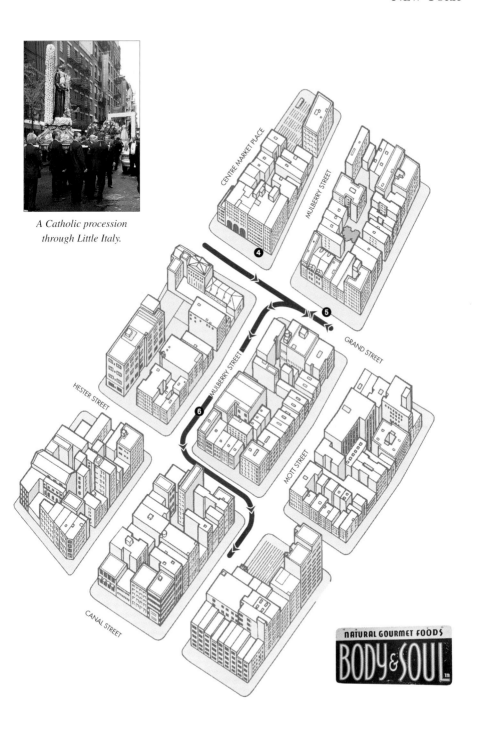

*A Catholic procession
through Little Italy.*

A GOURMET TRAIL: LITTLE ITALY AND CHINATOWN

Health conscious New Yorkers still love their food.

7 Negotiate your way past street venders selling soup, tofu and chicken feet from trolleys in **Mott Street**, the focus of old Chinatown. There are more than 100 gold Buddhas in the shopfront shrine of the **Eastern States Buddhist Temple,** at No. 64. Buy a fortune for a dollar or – for good luck with money – light a stick of incense to the Four-Faced Buddha.

8 The homely, pine-walled **Ice Cream Factory** at No. 65 Bayard Street serves flavours as diverse as lychee and pumpkin pie, as well as sorbets and milkshakes. The shops here sell anything from stationery to herbal medicine and the latest in plastic toys.

Between Mott and Mulberry Streets, notice the **Wall of Democracy** which is covered with newspapers giving information about the situation back in China.

9 At **Columbus Park,** hunched Chinese men slam down dimes over games of mah-jong while the women have their fortune told. There are chrysanthemum bushes and a baseball court on what was, at the beginning of the 19th century, the site of New York's worst slum. The run-down tenements here were known by names like Bandits' Roost while gangs like the Plug Uglies roamed the streets.

A traditional Chinese shop display.

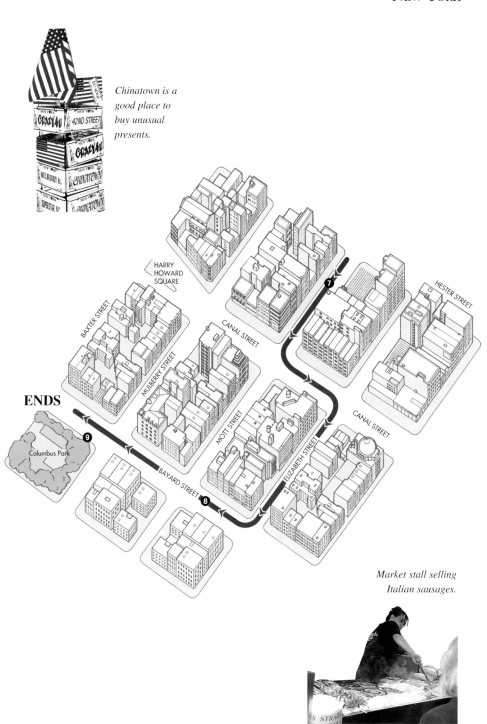

Chinatown is a good place to buy unusual presents.

HARRY HOWARD SQUARE

BAXTER STREET

MULBERRY STREET

CANAL STREET

7

HESTER STREET

ENDS

Columbus Park

9

MOTT STREET

ELIZABETH STREET

CANAL STREET

BAYARD STREET

8

Market stall selling Italian sausages.

On the Waterfront:
To South Street Seaport

► **STARTS**
Chambers Street and Centre
Street. Nearest subway:
Chambers Street and Centre
Street.

■ **ENDS:**
Fulton Fish Market. Nearest
subway: Fulton Street. Turn
left on to South Street
Viaduct, back to point (6),
following Fulton Street to
junction with William Street,
a five-minute walk.

' The place encircled by many swift tides and sparkling waters', wrote poet Walt Whitman of Manhattan. For unforgettable views of the island's skyline, follow in his footsteps across the iconic Brooklyn Bridge, which he described as 'the best, most effective medicine my soul has yet partaken'. From City Hall to the 'street of sails', walk along cobbled streets to an area steeped in seafaring and fishing traditions. Tourists swarm to an 11-block outdoor museum with galleries and historic ships, a shop-filled pier and a traditional fish market. Take to the water on a 19thC paddle steamer or one of the many vessels that ply the harbour of the island city. This is low-rise New York where the twisting streets are testament to the city's early random growth, a world away from the grid

*Sculpture outside
City Hall.*

system. The first section is deserted at the weekends but South Street Seaport is always lively.

City perspective from Brooklyn Bridge.

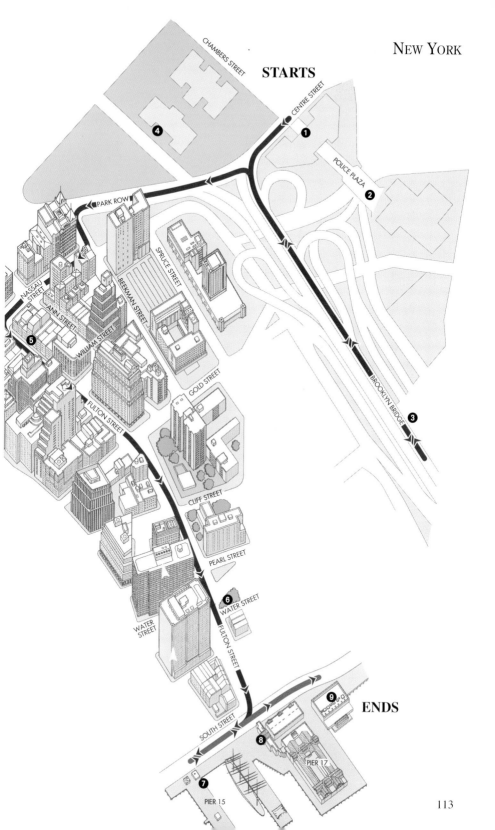

NEW YORK

STARTS

CHAMBERS STREET

CENTRE STREET

POLICE PLAZA

PARK ROW

NASSAU STREET

ANN STREET

WILLIAM STREET

BEEKMAN STREET

SPRUCE STREET

GOLD STREET

FULTON STREET

CLIFF STREET

PEARL STREET

WATER STREET

WATER STREET

FULTON STREET

BROOKLYN BRIDGE

SOUTH STREET

ENDS

PIER 17

PIER 15

113

❶ Couples come to the **Municipal Building** (1914) with its wedding-cake tower for production-line marriage services. The Italianate Old New York County Courthouse (1878) is often referred to as the 'Tweed Courthouse' because it was here that politician Boss Tweed siphoned off millions of pounds of public money in one of the country's biggest corruption scandals.

Manhattan's largest statue crowns the Municipal Building.

❷ At the beginning of Brooklyn Bridge, **Police Plaza** is marked by a giant mural of smiling officers in angelic poses who in a display of typical New York confidence call themselves 'the City's Finest'. You can join cops and federal agents for lunch at the Metropolitan Improvement Company on Madison and Pearl streets. **Pearl Street** takes its name from the mother of pearl that once paved its shoreline. At No. 375 the tower of the New York Telephone Company is a building with no people, just cables.

❸ Once on **Brooklyn Bridge's** walkway 18ft (5.5m) above the rumbling traffic, stay in the pedestrian lane, safe from speeding cyclists. When completed in 1883 it was the longest suspension bridge in the world, and the first to be made in steel; the twin Gothic arches standing as 277-ft (84.5-m) portals to the city. Plaques along its length give detailed information about the construction, which claimed 20 lives including John A. Roebling's, the engineer, and even identify some of the Hudson River's vessels. Manhattan Bridge and Williamsburg Bridge to the north are both longer, but built after Brooklyn Bridge. BMW is a mnemonic used to remember their sequence. The waterside area north of the bridge, with its sprawling lumber yards, is devoted largely to industry and shipping.

Self-promotion at Police Plaza.

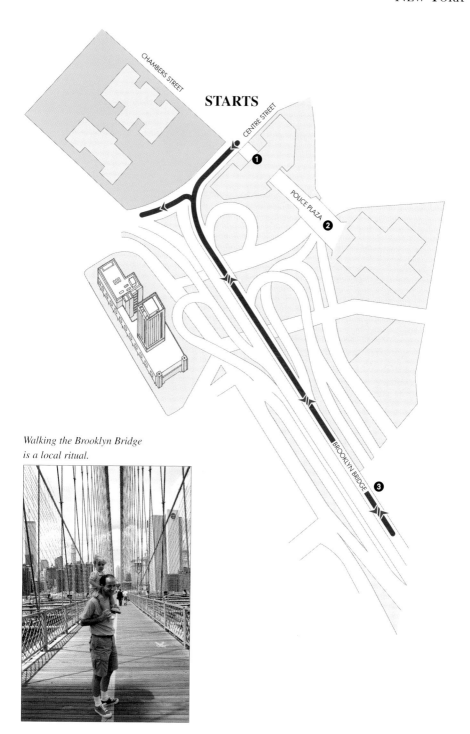

CHAMBERS STREET

STARTS

CENTRE STREET

❶

POLICE PLAZA

❷

BROOKLYN BRIDGE

❸

Walking the Brooklyn Bridge is a local ritual.

4 Return across the bridge to the courthouse on Park Row which is often mistaken for the less grand **City Hall**, seat of the city government. Protestors traditionally gather on the steps of the Georgian building, where visiting dignitaries are met by the mayor. It faces south because when it was built in 1812 the architects firmly believed the city wouldn't develop any further north. Newly renovated **City Hall Park** was once a cow pasture, before becoming New York's village green and the site of public executions. On a fine day, take a seat by the elegant fountain which is often surrounded by buskers. Two blocks north (off map) on Duane and Elk Streets is a graveyard only discovered in 1991 of more than 20,000 18thC African Americans, many of them thought to be involved in the anti-slave revolts of the time.

A star-spangled beast in Fulton Street.

City Hall Park is a surpisingly pleasant spot.

5 From Park Row, turn left on to Beekman Street, right down pedestrian Nassau Street and left on to **Fulton Street**. This area between City Hall Park and South Street Seaport is something of a no-man's land, unfortunately sandwiched between the gleaming renovations of its neighbours. Cheap clothes and tacky stationery is sold from the decrepit buildings which house some down-at-heel office space. A plaque on a building on Fulton Street just before Cliff Street marks the site of the first underground central station, and the origin of New York's current electrical system in 1882.

are at the start of the port area. Boat loads of sailors visited the brothels that once lined Water Street, and the whole area was until recently in general decline. Extensively redeveloped in the eighties, shops and restaurants in the reclaimed buildings make up the lively 'museum without walls' of **South Street Seaport** (open daily). Among the red-brick warehouses and counting houses of Schermerhorn Row (1812) are Sloppy Louie's, a popular fish restaurant, and a visitor's centre which has maps and all-inclusive tickets for the surrounding attractions.

6 When you have reached the **Titanic Memorial** on the corner of Fulton and Water Street, built as a lighthouse in memory of the victims of the doomed ship, you

The Titanic Memorial marks the start of South Street Seaport.

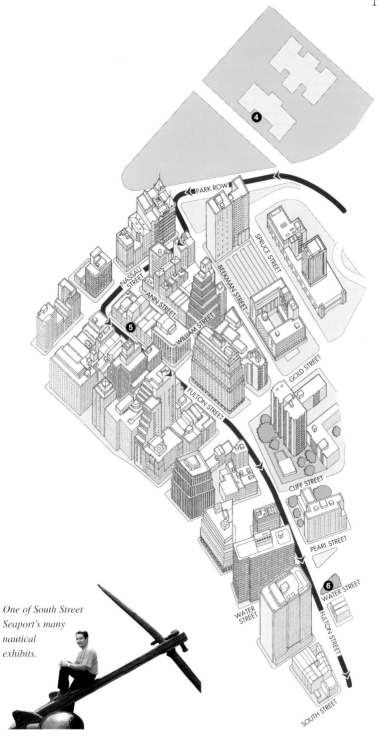

PARK ROW

SPRUCE STREET

NASSAU STREET

ANN STREET

BEEKMAN STREET

WILLIAM STREET

GOLD STREET

⑤

FULTON STREET

CLIFF STREET

PEARL STREET

⑥ WATER STREET

WATER STREET

FULTON STREET

SOUTH STREET

④

*One of South Street
Seaport's many
nautical
exhibits.*

117

On the Waterfront: To South Street Seaport

❼ Some 500 years after explorer Giovanni da Verrazano first sailed into the harbour, New York's maritime traditions are being kept alive. Turn right on to **South Street** where authentic wooden boats are built by craftsmen at the Boat Building Shop. At the Maritime Crafts Center at Pier 15 skilled workmen can be seen carving figureheads and making models.

❽ Brash **Pier 17** is always crowded with wandering tourists by day, and drinking bankers at night. Visitors mill around its indoor shopping centre, outdoor cafés, and waterside wooden terraces. A ship-like deck adjoining the third-floor food court gives great views of Brooklyn Bridge and across the river. Take a boat for panoramas of the city. This is how the immigrants arrived. Cruise the river on an old-fashioned paddle steamer, traditional schooner, a speedboat or tugboat which depart from Pier 17. From Battery Park (See World Traders, page 127) Circle Line cruises circumnavigate Manhattan in a three-hour trip and small popular ferry boats ply between the park, Ellis Island and the Statue of Liberty. Some provide commentaries or even lunch.

Performers in the 'living museum' of South Street Seaport.

A Fulton Street mime artist

❾ Walk behind Pier 17 to the **Fulton Fish Market** where fish have been sold for almost 200 years. Although the supplies are no longer hauled in from boats in the harbour, but delivered by refrigerated trucks, it is still worth seeing the action if you can get there before dawn – about 4 or 5am. The street and market is named after Robert Fulton, who developed the steamboat and whose Manhattan to Brooklyn ferry offices stood here. In the mid-1800s, the area was the focus for New York's thriving maritime commerce, where West Indian spices and rum and oil from the Atlantic were bought and sold.

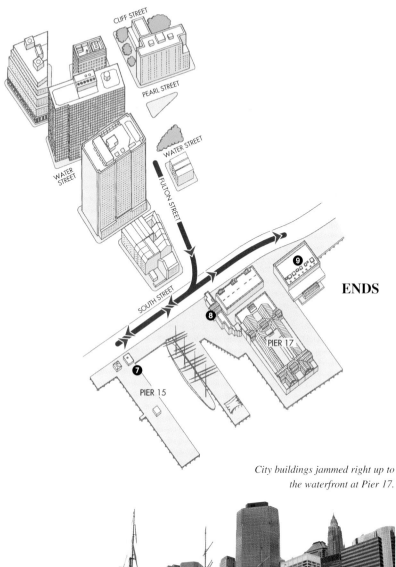

CLIFF STREET

PEARL STREET

WATER STREET

WATER STREET

FULTON STREET

SOUTH STREET

ENDS

9

8

7

PIER 17

PIER 15

City buildings jammed right up to the waterfront at Pier 17.

World Traders: Twin Towers to Battery Park

A bronze statue of George Washington at the head of Wall Street.

This walking tour guides you through Manhattan's southern tip, the birthplace of New York, for an ideal introduction to the city. Visit hidden churchyards and walk among ancient steeples of churches dwarfed by the Twin Towers of the World Trade Center. From the summit of the highest point of this soaring metropolis survey the sliver of land encircled by the waters that once made New York the world's busiest port. Visit the spot where the Dutch began their lucrative fur trading in 1625, and bought *Man-a-hatt-ta* from the Indians for a handful of beads and trinkets a year later. View the home of the Stock Exchange, where frenetic traders set the pace for the rest of the city. End where millions of hopefuls first set foot on 'the land of the free' at Battery Park and the gateway to the Statue of Liberty.

▶ **STARTS**
Broadway and Fulton Street. Nearest subway: Broadway and Fulton Street.

■ **ENDS**
Battery Park. Nearest subway: Bowling Green. Retrace your steps back to where State Street meets Broadway on the northern most tip of Battery Park.

Views of Ellis Island from Battery Park.

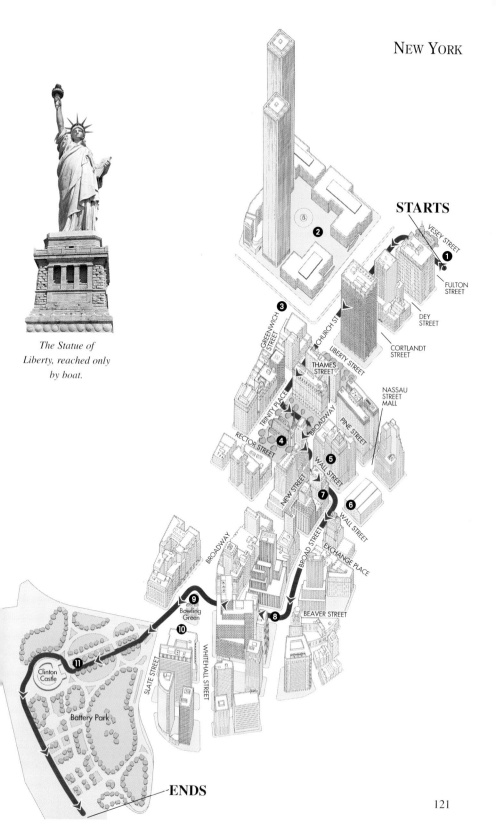

NEW YORK

The Statue of Liberty, reached only by boat.

STARTS

VESEY STREET

FULTON STREET

DEY STREET

CORTLANDT STREET

LIBERTY STREET

CHURCH ST

GREENWICH STREET

THAMES STREET

NASSAU STREET MALL

TRINITY PLACE

BROADWAY

PINE STREET

RECTOR STREET

WALL STREET

NEW STREET

WALL STREET

BROAD STREET

EXCHANGE PLACE

BROADWAY

BEAVER STREET

Bowling Green

WHITEHALL STREET

SLATE STREET

Clinton Castle

Battery Park

ENDS

1 Crumbling, tooth-like, black and white tombstones rise out of the green graveyard of **St Paul's Chapel**. New York's only pre-revolutionary building was built on a wheat field. The Hudson River which once flowed to its door has been long replaced with the teeming thoroughfare of Broadway. Inside is a pew dedicated to George Washington who was a worshipper here during the two years that New York was the national capital. There are daily services and noonday concerts on Mondays. Turn right down Fulton Street at the **Kalikow Building** which has more exterior columns than any other structure in the world.

2 Cross Church Street to join the tourists craning their necks and struggling to get the whole height of the 110-storey Twin Towers in the frame of their cameras at the **World Trade Center's** plaza. Take a seat among the fountains, flowers and sculptures that fill the centre of the 16-acre complex, supposedly covered with enough cement to build a pavement to Washington. Most of the visitors here have come to take the ear-popping express lift. It shoots to the world's highest open-air observation platform on the 110th floor in 58 seconds, bypassing the offices of 50,000 workers. Visit the Windows on the World (tel. 212 524 7000) restaurant in Tower One on the 107th floor for a reasonably priced if unatmospheric meal with views south of the city. It is advisable to book.

3 Traders of fresh produce sell flowers, bread, vegetables and bonsai trees on a welcome small scale at the junction of Greenwich and Liberty Streets. The **Farmers' Market**, dwarfed by the towers behind, takes place on Thursdays year-round and Tuesdays from April to December. Cross Church Street to the food stalls lining Liberty Plaza where tourists and office workers sit with chess players to eat open-air falafels and hot dogs. Look down Thames Street where a tiny bridge links Trinity building to the U.S. Realty building high across the street.

The colourful Georgian interior of St Paul's Chapel.

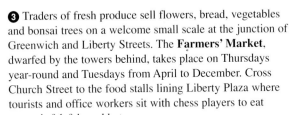

Street traders near the World Trade Center.

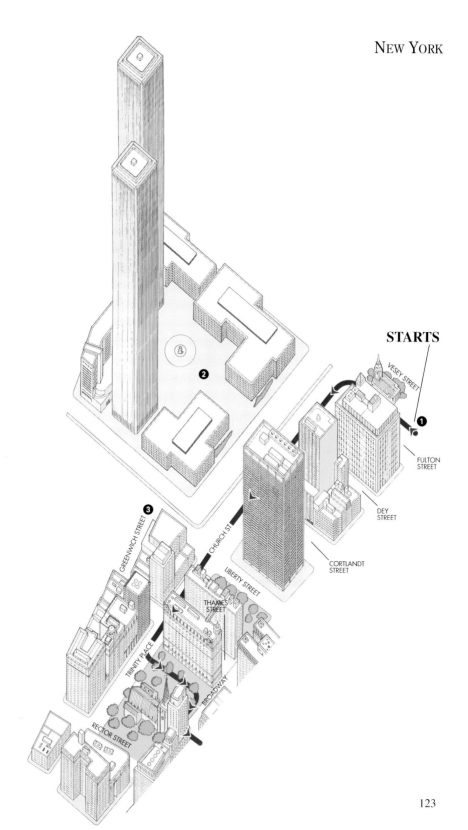

STARTS

VESEY STREET

❶

FULTON STREET

DEY STREET

❷

CORTLANDT STREET

CHURCH ST

LIBERTY STREET

❸

GREENWICH STREET

THAMES STREET

TRINITY PLACE

BROADWAY

RECTOR STREET

WORLD TRADERS: TWIN TOWERS TO BATTERY PARK

Robert Fulton's tombstone.

❹ Climb the gated steps between Pine and Rector Streets for a back door into the churchyard of **Trinity Church**. Its 280-ft (86-m) steeple, once the city's highest building, is now overshadowed by a crowd of skyscrapers. Join the visitors sitting under trees, heavy with blossom in spring, in a much more pleasant alternative to the concrete plazas. Wander among the weathered tombstones marking the graves of Robert Fulton, the inventor of the steamboat, and William Bradford, the founder of the first New York newspaper in 1725. Inside, where traders often pray, is a small gift shop and museum.

❺ Exit through the front of the church where its position at the head of **Wall Street** becomes clear. The surprisingly narrow thoroughfare is named after a 6-ft (1.8-m) high wooden defence the Dutch built in 1653 to protect themselves from warring Indians. 'The street' as locals call it, has been the centre of the city's financial dealings since traders met under a buttonwood tree here in 1792. Its buildings, appropriately, often look more like temples than banks.

Extra wide Broad Street was once a waterway.

❻ Early traders brought their European goods for inspection at **Federal Hall National Memorial** when it was the U.S. Customs House. The Greek Revival building now welcomes visitors with tours and exhibits about the Bill of Rights and the Constitution in rooms off the impressive Pantheon-inspired main rotunda. (Closed Sat, Sun.) A statue of George Washington, sworn in as the first American president on this site, surveys Broad Street.

New York Stock Exchange.

❼ There are free weekday visits to the **New York Stock Exchange** to view the daily trading of 200 million shares. Although computerization has lessened the drama, these tours of the heart of the global economy are extremely popular, so arrive as early as possible to get a ticket for later in the day. (Closed Sat, Sun.)

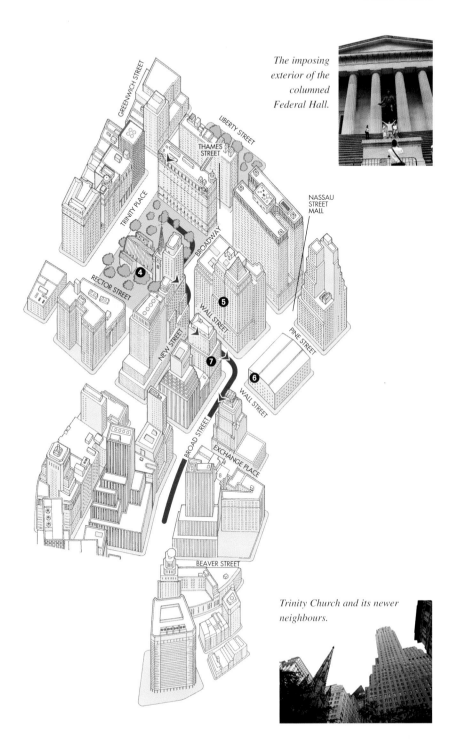

GREENWICH STREET

LIBERTY STREET

THAMES STREET

TRINITY PLACE

NASSAU STREET MALL

BROADWAY

RECTOR STREET

❹

❺

WALL STREET

NEW STREET

PINE STREET

❼

❻

WALL STREET

BROAD STREET

EXCHANGE PLACE

BEAVER STREET

The imposing exterior of the columned Federal Hall.

Trinity Church and its newer neighbours.

WORLD TRADERS: TWIN TOWERS TO BATTERY PARK

8 Continue down Broad Street. This unusually wide road was a canal before it was filled in the 17th century. Turn right down Beaver Street, its name a reminder of the animals once hunted here for their fur. At 28 Broadway the small basement **Museum of American Financial History** tells the story of the last century of Wall Street, where it costs two million dollars to become a Stock Exchange member. (Closed Sun, Mon.) Opposite, the **Cunard Building** once sold tickets for the Titanic and other big ocean liners. As the post office, today it sells stamps from the Great Hall.

Immigrant hopes captured in bronze in Battery Park.

9 Notice the stocky bronze **bull** at the head of **Bowling Green** park, patted by traders for luck. It was put outside the Stock Exchange one night as a joke by Italian sculptor Arturo DiModica before being moved to its current location. The small triangular park takes its name from the bowlers who rented it for one peppercorn in the 18th century.

A bullish market?

10 A photograph outside the **National Museum of the American Indian** is a gentle reminder that many of the early skyscrapers were built using the cheap labour of the Mohawk Indians. The museum, with its resource centre and workshops, works with American Indians to create a 'living museum' with contemporary art exhibits, and has an active policy of returning articles of tribal significance. Changing displays from a million artefacts spanning 10,000 years, including woven duck decoys from 200BC and exquisite beaded moccasins, reflect the spirituality the Indians invested in them. (Open daily.)

Finely crafted moccasins at the Native American Indian Museum.

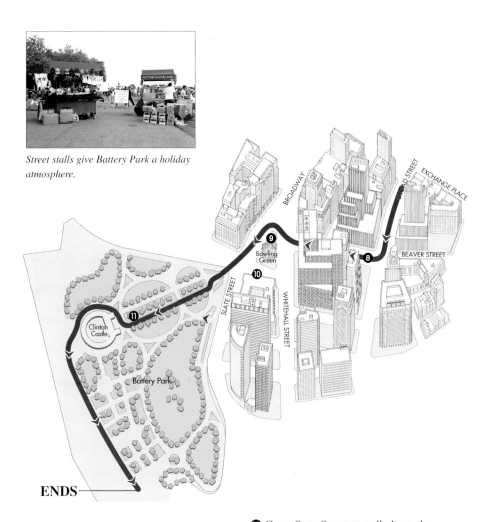

Street stalls give Battery Park a holiday atmosphere.

Watching the world go by in Battery Park.

⓫ Cross State Street to walk down the formal promenade in **Battery Park**. It leads to a sculpture dedicated to the immigrants who arrived at Castle Clinton often after harrowing journeys by boat. The low open circle of the sandstone 'castle', built as a fort, was the immigration office before Ellis Island and now acts as a ferry ticket office. The queues for boats to Ellis Island – with its moving museum of the 17 million immigrants who entered here between 1892 and 1954 – and the Statue of Liberty is a present-day reversal of the hopeful new arrivals waiting to be 'processed'.